Early Praise for From Day One

"Bill White's book should be required reading for anyone starting a career, and a must-read for anyone after they have started their career."

—**Warren Bennis, Distinguished Professor of Business Administration, University of Southern California, and co-author,** *Geeks and Geezers: How Era, Values, and Defining Moments Shape Leaders*

"If you are a young person who believes in the future, who believes in personal growth, who has the humility to learn, this book is for you."

—**From the foreword by Ram Charan, Charan Associates business advisor, speaker, and author of several bestselling books, including** *Confronting Reality* **and** *Execution: The Discipline of Getting Things Done*, **as well as several other books**

"Excellent, practical advice and wisdom-based counsel from someone who has been both in the trenches and at the peak. The perfect graduation and career kick-off gift."

—**Stephen R. Covey, author of** *The 7 Habits of Highly Effective People* **and** *The 8th Habit: From Effectiveness to Greatness*

"Looking for a shortcut to fame and fortune? This book won't satisfy. But if you want to know what you don't know that blocks your path to a dream career, you can do no better than putting your ear to Bill White's ground."

—**Allan Cox, management author and consultant to boards, CEOs, and top teams**

"Fortunate is the young professional—or old professional, for that matter—who heeds this advice. Its theme rings clear and true: Concern yourself with making your organization better and learning from every experience and everyone. As I read this book, the word that kept coming to my mind was *integrity*—having a life or moral code that is integrated into one's attitudes and behaviors at work. *From Day One* defines success at a much higher level; it empowers and implores people to choose the natural high road, and lets success follow. It is also filled with practical tips, not an idealist or moralist dream but a meat and potatoes success story!"

—Jean Egmon, President, Third Angle, Inc. and co-author of *The Prepared Mind of a Leader: Eight Skills Leaders Use to Innovate, Make Decisions, and Solve Problems*

"Benjamin Franklin, the patron saint of self-improvement books, coined the maxim 'doing well by doing good' in his *Poor Richard's Almanack*. Now, in this wonderfully readable book, Bill White shows, step by step, how you can indeed truly do well in your career by doing good in this world."

—From the foreword by Walter Isaacson, author of *Benjamin Franklin: An American Life*, President and CEO of the Aspen Institute, and Former Chairman and CEO of CNN

"*From Day One* is not a book of pie-in-the-sky platitudes. This is reality-based advice–tested, tempered, and proven by life experience—a 'toolbox' that will provide young professionals with the fundamental habits for career success. It's must reading for anyone who aspires to career success in business, industry, education, or government."

—Jack Rayman, Director of Career Services and Affiliate Professor of Counseling Psychology and Education, Penn State University

"Oh, what wisdom! These profound truths are rarely found in the world of academics. Yet they are the *only* truths that count in life, both personally and professionally. Savor every thought!"

—Glenna Salsbury, author of *The Art of The Fresh Start*, professional speaker, and past President, National Speakers Association

"*From Day One* is a great primer to assist college students today in making a successful move to the world of work. For young professionals, *From Day One* is a valuable tool to help understand the nuances of working for a corporation and how to better prepare themselves for this journey. I wish I had such a guide when I was embarking on my career journey. However, I will make sure my three children not only read it, but take notes on how to become a valuable employee."

—Paul G. Schneider, Scherer Schneider Paulick, counseling and outplacement firm

"Overflowing with tips, wisdom, and solid values on which to build your career...and your life. Although written for making the most of your first job, it's valuable for people at any level wanting to do better for their organizations and themselves."

—Ed Zschau, visiting lecturer, Princeton University, and former member of the U.S. House of Representatives (CA)

From Day One

From Day One

Success Secrets for Starting Your Career

William J. White

PEARSON PRENTICE HALL
AN IMPRINT OF PEARSON EDUCATION

Upper Saddle River, NJ • Boston • Indianapolis • New York • London
San Francisco • Toronto • Sydney • Tokyo • Singapore • Hong Kong
Cape Town • Madrid • Paris • Milan • Munich • Amsterdam

Vice President and Editor-in-Chief: Tim Moore
Acquisitions Editor: Paula Sinnott
Editorial Assistant: Susie Abraham
Development Editor: Russ Hall
Director of Marketing: John Pierce
International Marketing Manager: Tim Galligan
Cover Designer: Chuti Praserstith
Managing Editor: Gina Kanouse
Copy Editor: Cheryl Lenser
Indexer: Cheryl Lemmens
Compositor: Jake McFarland
Manufacturing Buyer: Dan Uhrig

© 2006 by Pearson Education, Inc.
Publishing as Prentice Hall
Upper Saddle River, New Jersey 07458

Prentice Hall offers excellent discounts on this book when ordered in quantity for bulk purchases or special sales. For more information, please contact U.S. Corporate and Government Sales, 1-800-382-3419, corpsales@ pearsontechgroup.com. For sales outside the U.S., please contact International Sales, 1-317-581-3793, international@pearsontechgroup.com.

Library of Congress Cataloging-in-Publication Data is on file.
Printed in the United States of America

ISBN 0-13-138228-4
This product is printed digitally on demand.
Pearson Education Ltd.
Pearson Education Australia Pty., Limited
Pearson Education South Asia Pte. Ltd.
Pearson Education Asia Ltd.
Pearson Education Canada, Ltd.
Pearson Educación de Mexico, S.A. de C.V.
Pearson Education——Japan
Pearson Education Malaysia, Pte. Ltd.

DEDICATION

To General Georges Doriot, Professor Harvard Business School (1926-1966), whose inspiration and approach to life still lives in all his students!

Contents

ACKNOWLEDGMENTS

From the initial concept to publication, a great many people influenced and contributed to this book in a positive way.

First, I want to thank the thought leaders and executives who graciously shared their thoughts and ideas with me: Peggy Barr, John C. Bogle, William Bowen, Herman Cain, James Citrin, Donald P. Delves, Andrea Jung, Frank LaFasto, Pamela Forbes Lieberman, Robert Kelley, Greg Maddux, Nell Minow, Gerry Niewoehner, Thomas O. Ryder, and Edmund J. Wilson.

Also sharing their words and wisdom were two long-term and steadfast mentors and bosses, Warren Batts and John D. Gray. Their advice over the years proved invaluable to me at the time, and they contributed to this book in numerous ways beyond being interviewed.

Other "bosses" who greatly influenced my philosophy and style included Edgar Stoval at Mead and Robert Bass at Bell & Howell.

I am indebted to Northwestern University's former dean, Jerry Cohen, who first gave me the chance to teach, and to Robert Landel, who taught me how at the University of Virginia's Darden School of Business. My faculty associates in the Industrial Engineering & Management Science Department of Northwestern University provided the environment where the ideas for this book came to life. Jerry Kirschenbaum, a Northwestern classmate, gave me the encouragement to try to actually write a book.

Paula Sinnott at Pearson Prentice Hall shared my enthusiasm for this book and had the commitment to make it a reality, while making valuable suggestions for its improvement.

My ghostwriter, Tricia Crisafulli, "got" the idea from the very first. Her business insights, speedy work, and encouragement made the writing tasks enjoyable and very satisfying.

My family's support, particularly that of my wife, Jane, was invaluable. Jane never wavered in her enthusiasm for my project, always responding eagerly to my frequent request of "Would you please read this?" She is the love of my life, and I cannot thank her enough for her support, inspiration, humor, gentleness, and caring.

Throughout my career, I have relied on Jane's strength, wisdom, and perceptiveness. I'm lucky that my close, trusted advisor is someone I live with. Together, we've had enormous joy being parents to our sons, Jim and Tom, and our daughters, Mia and Gretchen. My hope is that our grandchildren—Benjamin, Slater, Bill, Stuart, Brian, Brigid, Patrick, Amy, Maggie, Cutter, Colin, Mary Jane, and Eleanor—will find this book valuable when they are approaching their life career choices. Looking back, I appreciate the love I've received from my family. I can honestly say that my faith, support of my children and family, and wonderful friends have allowed me to keep things in perspective.

ABOUT THE AUTHOR

William J. White has been a professor in the McCormick School of Engineering and Applied Science at Northwestern University in Evanston, Ill. since January 1998. He is the recipient of several teaching awards, including the Alumni Association's Award for Excellence in Teaching. He also teaches at the distinguished Kellogg School of Management.

Mr. White served as chairman, CEO, and president of Bell & Howell Company (now Proquest Company). Previously, he was chairman and president of Whitestar Graphics, Inc., and prior to that he was executive vice president and a director of USG Corporation. He also held executive positions at Masonite Corporation, Mead Corporation, and Hartmarx Corporation.

Mr. White is an industrial engineering graduate of Northwestern University and he received an MBA degree from Harvard University. He coauthored *Creative Collective Bargaining*, published by Prentice Hall in 1965.

He has been the chairman of the Advisory Council of the McCormick School of Engineering and Applied Science at Northwestern University. He is past chairman of the Business Advisory Council at the University of Illinois at Chicago.

Mr. White is a trustee of Northwestern University, as well as a member of the Board of Directors of Packaging Dynamics Corporation, The Reader's Digest Association, Evanston Northwestern Healthcare, The Illinois Mathematics and Science Academy Foundation, and The Field Museum.

FOREWORD

BY RAM CHARAN

As a young person, you are entering a world that will always change. Some young people have courage, stamina, and the temperament to do more than just accept the change. They lead the change. They have an insatiable appetite to learn what is happening, to seek new ideas, to look at the world from a historical perspective, and to talk to people who have learned from history. They distill wisdom and learn what not to do. They recognize what lies ahead and what will demand the best of their mental faculties and behaviors—knowing that their actions will inspire others.

If you are a young person who believes in the future, who believes in personal growth, who has the humility to learn, this book is for you.

I have known Bill White for a long time. Throughout his life, his values have served him very well. At Harvard, he sought out instructors who had wisdom, built character, and shared experiences. Professor Georges Doriot was one of those instructors. He was legendary. He helped build the character of many CEOs. Remember, no young person knows everything: What they do not know, they learn from people with wisdom. At Harvard, Bill was one of those people. In the early days of his career, he went "where the action is," which was on the ground floor. He built up his life and career from there. What Bill accomplished for himself was not what mattered most to him. Rather, it was helping others accomplish their goals and beyond, and rejoicing in their success, that has always been of utmost importance to Bill. If these qualities resonate with you, then you've picked up the right book.

Every single day is the first step of the next portion of your life. Be a marathon player, not a sprinter. Have the temperament, stamina, and patience to know when to make a change and when to remain the same. Bill provides a stellar example for living this life.

This is a small book. Read it carefully. Discuss it with your colleagues. Internalize the gems that it holds. Remember the importance of doing good. How you live will contribute to your generation. True success is achieving both your ambitions and your happiness— find the balance. The world needs you.

Ram Charan, Charan Associates business advisor, speaker, and author of several bestselling books, including *Confronting Reality* and *Execution: The Discipline of Getting Things Done*, as well as several other books

FOREWORD

BY WALTER ISAACSON

Many people starting a new career focus on one thing: how to get ahead. Later in their careers, they learn the importance of other goals, such as making a contribution, upholding values, and pursuing a passion that they find meaningful.

Throughout his distinguished career as a major business executive, professor, and corporate board leader, Bill White has developed a crucial leadership insight that is valuable for aspiring young people as they start their careers—and also for the business community and world at large. Bill knows that goals and values are an integral component of being truly successful.

To the extent that you focus on making a contribution rather than getting ahead, you will rise naturally in a company. Your success will be seen as based on merit and worth. Your company and colleagues will all benefit from your rise, and they will be eager to help someone they perceive as helpful to others.

In the previous generation, some saw ruthlessness and greed as being methods for getting ahead. We all saw where that led and what it did to corporate America.

In today's business world a premium is placed on values—and rightly so. Corporations treasure integrity and credibility, and will promote the people they trust and who can guard their corporate values.

Your personal ethics are reflected, and shaped, by the dozens of little decisions you make each day. What this book shows is why it is so important these days to get this aspect of your career right.

The natural temptation for ambitious young workers is to look at a situation and say, "What can I get out of it?" True success, however, comes from knowing how to lead by serving. When you serve the larger goals of your organization, the people around you, and the greater good of your society, you are more likely to get ahead and build a fulfilling, rewarding career.

Benjamin Franklin, the patron saint of self-improvement books, coined the maxim "doing well by doing good" in his *Poor Richard's Almanac*. Now, in this wonderfully readable book, Bill White shows, step-by-step, how you can indeed truly do well in your career by doing good in this world.

Walter Isaacson, author of *Benjamin Franklin: An American Life*, President and CEO of the Aspen Institute, and Former Chairman and CEO of CNN

INTRODUCTION

As a corporate-executive-turned-college-professor, I've seen the business world from many perspectives. Much of what I impart in these pages reflects my own career. My goal is to provide practical wisdom that will allow you to benefit from the experience of others. I'm honored in these pages to pass on the knowledge, observations, and perspective of many executives and thought leaders, who have generously shared from their own careers (including when they were just starting out), as well as their interactions with young professionals.

They include Jack Bogle, founder of The Vanguard Group; Chicago Cubs pitcher Greg Maddux; Andrea Jung, chairman of Avon Products and #3 on the *Wall Street Journal*'s list of "The Top 50 Women to Watch," and Herman Cain, an African-American businessman who rose from humble roots in Georgia to the top ranks of corporate America.

The dozen or so individuals I've interviewed have titles such as chairman, CEO, president, and vice president. They have achieved levels of success that many people yearn for throughout their careers. As a college student or a young professional, you may have your sights set on the executive suite some day. Given that ambition, wouldn't you want to learn from the experiences of those who have already made it? Wouldn't you want to benefit from their wisdom as well as from their mistakes? Of course you would.

My aim in this book is to help you—whether you're a college student, recent graduate, graduate student, or young professional in the first five years of your career—shorten your learning curve. The faster you can learn these secrets of success and incorporate them into your professional life, the more quickly you'll become a highly valued member of your organization.

While each person's experience is and should be unique, I believe there are important commonalities to success. I see them as a mosaic of behaviors, practices, and attitudes, which will be discussed throughout the book. Therefore, you may want to apply some of these suggestions immediately and implement others later. What's important for you is to discover what resonates for you right now, see what works, and then add more skills and habits over time.

I remember what it was like, many years ago, to join a corporation with big ideas and high expectations but little practical knowledge of how things really work. A few years later, I learned what it was like to be a manager, hiring new people and coaching and developing internal talent. Later, I became an executive, including chairman and CEO of a New York Stock Exchange-traded company, and was the steward of corporate resources, values, and talent. Now, in my latest role, as a professor at the McCormick School of Engineering and Applied Science at Northwestern University, I have the day-to-day experience of teaching and advising students who want to be prepared for the future.

Students often ask me, "How do I get started on the job? What should I do the first week? What do I have to know? What should I read?"

You can Google all you want. You can find tips and hints on how to write a dynamite résumé and ace an interview. But you still won't know how to be successful in your career—from Day One. Thus, when my students ask me to recommend a book on this subject, after much research I decided to write my own, based on observations, anecdotes, surveys, speeches, articles, and readings accumulated over my long career.

Foremost among the lessons in these pages is the importance of making a contribution. As you will learn throughout this book, the best strategy for a young professional, a seasoned manager, or even a top executive is to make the best possible contribution to the company or organization. This may sound counterintuitive, particularly if you're a college student or a recent graduate who is used to competing with and challenging others. Trust me on this one. Based on my own experience and what I've seen in the corporate arena, when you focus on the company's goals first, you'll produce a meaningful return in the long run. And you'll be a success.

True success stems from feeling good about your accomplishments and knowing that you're making a difference in your company or organization. Ultimately, this will be the legacy you leave behind in every job and in every organization throughout your career. Starting out, however, you may be most concerned about financial rewards, which are certainly important. What too few people understand, particularly as they launch their careers, is that you must make a difference *first*; then you have a greater chance of achieving financial rewards in the future. The more you contribute, the more challenging positions will be offered to you with bigger salaries and bonuses attached. This payoff over the long term doesn't mean that you have to wait for great things to happen. From Day One you can reap the satisfaction that comes from making a contribution and establish a firm footing on the path to true success.

At this point, you may be saying, "Okay, okay. I'll make a contribution. But first, I've got to find a job. Where are the hot jobs? What should I be doing?" If those are the questions you're asking, you're in good company. I hear them all the time from my students. However, these questions, are not the ones you should be asking.

What I do with my students is turn the questions around. "What do you get excited about? What are your passions? What activities engage you so much that you can hardly believe the time went by?" If you aren't passionate about what you do, you will feel as if you're behind the pack. You're likely to be frustrated, which can damage your relationships with co-workers, associates, and even the people closest to you. You owe it to yourself to identify your passions early and follow them wherever they lead you.

This is a different approach than many students take. They are eager to get out into the working world, or they are acutely aware of the expectations of parents and grandparents who want a return on their emotional and financial investment in four-plus years of college. Believe me, I understand those pressures! But a world of difference exists between "a job" and "the right job." Your first job and your relationship with your first boss (good or bad) will set the tone for much of your working life. If you have a positive experience, the confidence gained and favorable feedback received will last for many years. If it's negative, you may feel tainted for as many years.

Maybe you're still not convinced that you should be spending all this time *thinking* about your career instead of jumping into job searches and résumé writing. Consider something that happened to me many years ago when I was starting my career. I was a co-op student at Northwestern University, which meant that instead of going to school for four years, I put in five, including a year-and-a-half of work experience over several quarters at S.C. Johnson in Racine, Wis. During my work experience there, I was encouraged to meet with the company's industrial psychologist, which was a rare experience in those days, particularly for a 19-year-old intern. The psychologist put me through a battery of tests, which he then analyzed. I can still remember his sitting down with me to discuss the results.

"Bill," he said, "let me tell you the bad news first. You're really not outstanding in anything. But the good news is, you're pretty good at a lot of things. From a career standpoint, you should think about being a generalist—a general manager, for example."

That insight planted a seed and helped me set a goal. Of course, having a goal is one thing; achieving it is quite another. I was helped considerably when I enrolled in the Harvard MBA program in 1961. While there, I became a student of the late Georges Doriot, a legendary professor whose lessons went far beyond the process and philosophy of management. Among the many things he taught was how to get started on our careers and, more importantly, how to think about our careers. His lessons remained with me throughout my professional life, and they still ring true today. Once you were a "Doriot student," you remained so for life. I am honored to be in this group of esteemed peers.

Lastly, in my career, I've been fortunate to hold some interesting job assignments that allowed me not only to manage people but also to teach them. In fact, my style of management is very much that of a coach and teacher. My philosophy always has been that by teaching someone, I could make that individual better at his or her job. Thus, by passing on what I knew, by sharing from my own expertise, I could leverage my skills and knowledge to reap a greater return for the company.

Now it's your turn to benefit from the wisdom and experience of others and insights into achieving long-term happiness and true success as you begin from Day One.

PART I:
WHAT YOU NEED TO KNOW

1

1

WHAT CONTRIBUTION WILL YOU MAKE?

"People who do well in life understand things that other people don't understand."

—Georges Doriot

A distinct difference exists between what you know and what you understand. You probably know a great many things based on the courses you've taken and what you've learned thus far. Understanding, however, comes mostly from time and experience.

Whether you're entering college, you've just graduated, or you are in the first few years of your professional career, you are gaining valuable experiences that contribute to your lifelong "understanding curve." As you face challenges in your personal life and your academic or professional career, you are beginning to apply what you've learned to situations as they occur. You will make your share of mistakes. If you learn from your mistakes, you will benefit a great deal. If you can learn from the mistakes of others, however, you will leapfrog ahead on the "understanding curve."

Executives, leaders, and superstars in their field have truly "made it" when it comes to professional and personal success. They are at the pinnacle of their careers. Some of their experiences, like mine, span two generations. Their wisdom, however, is timeless, particularly as companies reinforce many of their core values.

Companies are stressing the importance of delivering value to all constituents—not just stockholders, but also employees, suppliers, and customers. At the same time, companies are vastly different than they were 30, 40, or 50 years ago. Technology has enabled greater connectivity, opening new markets and opportunities while allowing people to work in a number of different ways, from flextime to telecommuting—all at a much greater speed. You're the beneficiary of this change. In this day and age, you are leading my generation in utilizing new technology. Who knows what technological inroads will be made in the future that will change the way we work even more!

So what does that mean to you, the college student or young professional? I firmly believe it has everything to do with you, both as you start your career and as you move through the ranks to become a young manager and maybe an executive some day. To do this, you will need not only technical knowledge, but leadership skills as well. The kind of leadership I'm talking about is based on ethical behavior and recognizing the value of everyone who is involved in the organization, including the employees, the customers, and the stockholders. Above all, you must discover and follow your passion, because this is truly what will carry you forward in your career.

Managing Your Career from Day One

People often ask, "What is the secret to being successful?" Some of them, I'm sure, don't like the answer at first. The best way to manage your career, from Day One, is to focus on the contribution you will make to your employer. In other words, it's not about you. It's about what you can do to further the goals of your company or organization. Admittedly, this type of thinking changes the rules of the game from a contest to be won today into a long-term investment in which you are an integral player.

"Wait a minute," you're probably thinking. "I'm not signing on for the Peace Corps or joining some 'serve-the-greater-good' organization. I want to get a job, earn money (preferably lots of it), and get ahead. Isn't that what I went to college for?"

The short answer is yes and no. You can jump on the fast track, catch the brass ring, climb the ladder, and all the other clichés of achievement. But you still may not be successful. Real success stems from the satisfaction of knowing that your work is important, that what you do makes a difference. This runs contrary to what you see on television and read in the press—that success is all about becoming the survivor as a result of climbing over, beating up, outmaneuvering, and manipulating your competition. That's not how it is in the real world. Effective businesses are collaborative, cooperative, and team-oriented. If you think the way to win is to annihilate the competition, you're the one who will ultimately be the loser.

Consider the advice of one of the most accomplished executives who ever occupied a corner office: John C. "Jack" Bogle, founder and former chairman of The Vanguard Group. He outlined for young professionals what he calls his two rules for success: "Rule Number 1: Get out of bed in the morning. Get up and get going. Go through the day, and do the right things. Work hard at your job. Do everything you're asked to do and more. Don't worry about what's going to happen ten years from now; focus on getting through the day. I never thought about wanting to be a VP. I was a one-day guy."

"Rule Number 2," he added, "is to repeat Rule Number 1 all over again the next day."[1]

Human nature being what it is, however, most people tend to focus too much on the near future and emphasize their goals and objectives to get a better job, to get a promotion, to get a raise, and so forth. Most people fail to understand that their ability to make a meaningful and measurable contribution will distinguish them within a company or organization. The goal, therefore, is to apply yourself— your talent, energy, and ideas—to accomplishing the company's goals. Then you will have the satisfaction of knowing you made a difference, and you will greatly increase your chances of achieving your personal objectives as well. It will be a win-win for you and for the company.

Putting others first, ahead of individual accomplishment or self-aggrandizement, is a valued quality in all endeavors, but it's rarely found in some. In professional sports, from women's soccer to the National Football League, in which a few high achievers are elevated to superstar status, it's rarer still. One of the exceptions is Greg Maddux of the Chicago Cubs, a low-key man of high accomplishment, including becoming only the 22nd major-league pitcher to reach 300 career victories. A future Hall of Famer who has won four National League Cy Young Awards, Greg is a star in the world of professional athletics, which you may think is far removed from the corporate arena. Yet, the same attributes of excellence that he embodies are what make someone successful in the business world: working hard, studying the situation, analyzing the alternatives, and always looking to make a contribution to the team's greater good.

Greg's philosophy for putting the team first applies to young people starting their careers: "I realize that without the other 24 guys on the team, I wouldn't have a job. If the team does well, you're most likely doing well." In the corporate world, as in sports, hotshots exist who are clearly most interested in their own gains, even if it's at the expense of the team. From his perspective, Greg has the following advice, which applies equally to the corporations and the sporting teams: "You can't control the efforts that others are putting in. The important thing is that the people around you see that you are doing everything that you can. So be as good as you can be. Remember, talk is cheap, so don't tell them—show them."[2]

By emphasizing the team first—whether in baseball or at a company—you put your focus on the greater good of the organization. Admittedly, when you are just starting out it may be tricky to identify just how you can contribute to the organization's larger goals. It's not about trying to make a big splash or getting to the next level quickly. Rather, it's about understanding the organization's goals and aligning your efforts with them based on your own knowledge, skills, and expertise—even your personality.

Making a Contribution at Any Level

Most likely your first job as a recent college graduate will be very narrowly defined. You may be someone's assistant or a junior member of a team. It may seem that you're doing more watching and learning than actual doing in the first few days. Don't be discouraged! Even in this limited context, you can make a difference.

Not only is it okay to excel in the small things, it's essential. Unless you can prove yourself within the context of your assignments and everyday responsibilities, you won't be given larger and more significant tasks and projects. If you disdain your job as beneath you, or you think some tasks shouldn't be assigned to someone with your academic credentials, think again: Nobody is made a manager unless he's been a good team player, and I've never met anyone who was promoted because he complained bitterly about what he was doing every day.

Granted, as a new employee, your day-to-day tasks won't involve major changes to the organization. But if you do your required tasks in the best way possible, you will not only be positively noticed for your efforts, you will be accepted more quickly into the organization.

As you look to your professional future, ask yourself: What contribution do you want to make to *everyone*—not just to those you think are important? If you've already started working, take a look around you. What can you do for others? Can you give a hand to someone in your department occasionally, such as helping figure out a project? Does someone need coaching on a presentation? Can you help him with a technical problem with his computer? These are tangible ways in which you can contribute to the greater good and not expect anything in return.

As Jack Bogle advises, "Try to contribute to the knowledge, happiness, and welfare of the people around you—your colleagues, those who work for you, and those with whom you work. This is all 'bread-and-butter' stuff about living a good life and doing what it is you're supposed to be doing."[3]

This attitude of making a contribution is not only altruistic; it's also strategic. Robert E. Kelley, Ph.D., who teaches at Carnegie Mellon's Graduate School of Industrial Administration and consults with major companies, has studied the attitudes and behaviors of "star performers," who are also the subject of his book *How to Be a Star at Work: Nine Breakthrough Strategies You Need to Succeed.* From Day One, he advises, young professionals need to establish themselves as willing to help others and make a contribution to their team, their department, and their company.

"It's important to help out others early on, in particular those people you are going to be working with, either in your work group or those who are next to your work group," Robert said. "This sends a number of messages—first of all, that you are a 'giver.' It also tells people that you know how the game is played, that work is not a solo activity."

Those who don't understand these unwritten rules of the workplace may be in for a rude awakening when, at some point, they have to turn to others for help or direction. "The first time they go to the network, they are going to get labeled as a 'taker,' as opposed to a 'giver,'" he added.

Even a new employee without much expertise can establish a reputation as a helpful person by sincerely offering assistance to others. "It's allowing other people to offload some work onto you when they are very busy," Robert continued. "All you have to say is, 'I can see you are under the gun. Can I do anything to help you out?' That is the first step. The second step is to think about all the things that you know about, which may or may not be directly related to your work, but which could be useful to someone else."[4]

Your contribution is not defined only by what you do. It's also impacted by your attitude and how you treat others. Are you a know-it-all trying to impress people with your knowledge, or are you a respectful listener trying to gain understanding? You can't fake this to win people over. You have to believe in making a contribution for it to become the foundation of your actions and behaviors. Over time, it will be the unconscious influence in how you approach any situation. On a conscious level, it will also help you make career choices that may be against the grain, but that could lead you to better opportunities in the future. Some of those opportunities may be at companies that initially appear to be less than desirable.

Pamela Forbes Lieberman, former president and chief executive officer of TruServ (now known as True Value Company), a cooperative principally of hardware stores, spent time with her team turning around this quality company that has faced difficulties and challenges. She recognized that this situation provided a unique opportunity for young professionals.

"We'd bring people in and say, 'Here are all our issues. But this is where we're going.' Then we'd invite them to be part of the team that gets us there," Pamela explained. "We'd say to them, 'Won't it be exhilarating to see where we'll go from here?' For these young professionals, it is a résumé-building opportunity."[5]

These opportunities may not be the most glamorous jobs. They may involve a turnaround situation, or a company that new management is trying to revive or take in a different direction. Being at the company at that particular point in time, you will be part of the team that turns the organization around. Your payback in the process may not be the immediate satisfaction of a fancy title at a hot company. You'll have to wait for your gratification, which in time will make it all the better.

"I was given some advice that changed my life and my career, which was to follow your compass, not your clock. Choose the company, not the title and not the money," said Andrea Jung, chairman of Avon Products.[6]

"That advice changed who I am, where I am. I did not always take the job with the most money. I always took the job because in my heart I knew it was the company and the purpose of that company that I believed in," added Andrea, who ranks as Number 3 on the *Wall Street Journal's* 2004 "Top 50 Women to Watch."[7]

The Value of Delayed Gratification

As you launch your career, sometimes the ideal job for you will not be the one that pays the best or has the most "bragging rights" among your friends, family, and peers. You may choose to work for a low salary today because you will gain valuable experience that will lead to a higher salary later. As a younger person, you can make that trade-off because, presumably, your financial burdens are less than they will be when you are 35 or 45.

The question to ask yourself now is, can you delay gratification—particularly if it means going without a new car for another year or two or living at home instead of on your own—to establish a better future? Would you choose a job where you can make a greater contribution over one that seems more impressive? What if the payoff for delaying gratification turns out to be a highly strategic move for your future? That would make that less-than-glamorous job more appealing, wouldn't it?

Sound Advice and Delayed Rewards

In my own career, I passed up an opportunity to be part of a very hot company to become a tailor—with a Harvard MBA—at a well-established firm. Here's how it happened: When I was in my MBA program, I actively sought out companies, particularly smaller ones, and I interviewed with recruiters who came to school. Then a friend told me about a great company in California that he thought we should both talk to and offered to set up interviews there for both of us. With the interviews arranged, we got on a plane to talk to this company I had not heard of—Mattel. This toy manufacturer, founded in 1945, made mostly conventional toys until 1959, when it launched the Barbie doll.

When I met with the people at Mattel, you could feel the pulse of the activity. The interviewer told me, "This place is growing so fast, if you sit still you can see the walls expand."

I left there with the conviction that, if Mattel made me an offer, I would take it. On my way back to Boston, I had a stopover in Chicago to meet with the management of Hart Schaffner & Marx (now Hartmarx Corporation), a very conservative clothing manufacturer, for my senior project. It was at that meeting that I first met John D. "Jack" Gray, who had recently become chairman and CEO of the company. After another Harvard MBA student and I had finished interviewing Jack about the company, he said to us, "We're looking for young people like you. If you'd like to interview with the company, I hope you'll consider coming back."

We thanked him for the offer but in so many words told him "no thanks."

Back in Boston I told my wife, Jane, about this exciting opportunity at Mattel, assuring her that this would be the most fantastic thing. Always the trusted advisor, Jane listened patiently to all of it and then said, "I think you should think about Hart Schaffner & Marx. At Mattel there is going to be a lot of competition from some very intelligent and ambitious people. But at Hart Schaffner & Marx, they won't have any other new MBAs on staff to compare you to. You'll really be able to get noticed there."

Taking her advice, I did go back to Hart Schaffner & Marx to interview. The opportunity was clear. I would become the first MBA the company had hired in at least a decade. But instead of working in a corner office, I'd have to spend quite a bit of time in the factories, learning every step of the tailoring process from basting to sewing to pressing. Without that hands-on experience, I wouldn't have any insight into how to make the operation more efficient, improve margins, and so forth.

In the end, I had three offers to consider: one from Mattel, one from Hart Schaffner & Marx, and one from Procter & Gamble, where I had worked after graduating from Northwestern University and in the summer while I was at Harvard. I discussed the situation with my mentor and advisor, Professor Doriot. "There is no question," he told me. "The long-term opportunity is better at Hart Schaffner & Marx. It's a good company with a great reputation."

I turned down Mattel and went to work for Hart Schaffner & Marx. My reasons were clear: I hoped to have an opportunity to utilize my newly acquired skills and knowledge, which would benefit the company, while growing rapidly within the organization. Over the next three years, half of my time was spent in the shop learning to become a tailor. My finished product was my own suit that I made myself, which I still have. At the end of four years, I was made a vice president responsible for several thousand people.

The moral of this story is simple: I decided to delay my gratification and gave up the job at the "hot company." Instead, by listening to my trusted advisors, I chose the company where I could learn more and make a bigger contribution. When I got my reward, it was a significant one. I received a vice president's title far more quickly than I would have elsewhere.

Goals, Ambition, and the Greater Good

All of us have goals and ambition. Focusing on the greater good doesn't mean you don't care if you ever get promoted or receive a raise in pay. Of course you have ambition and want to get ahead! But like much in life, this requires a balance. You can focus on the greater good, helping your company achieve its goals, while availing yourself of opportunities that will also help advance your career. The key is what comes first. If you lead with your own ambition, so that everything you do is about you, you'll short-circuit your own success.

Warren Batts has enjoyed an impressive career. He has led numerous companies, including Premark and Tupperware as CEO, and he has served on the boards of 14 major public companies. After working for a few years, he finished college at 29 and received an MBA in 1963. He took his first CEO post in 1967. That's a fast track by anybody's standards. So how did he do it?

Warren had goals and ambition, but he kept them in check by focusing first on what he could do at the organization. "Remember, people are much more willing to help you succeed if ambition isn't dripping from every pore. We all have ambition, but there are people who spend every single moment thinking of themselves and how is this going to help them get ahead," Warren remarked. "With people like that, the organization usually rises up and prevents them from getting ahead or finds a way to slow them down. So if you are always worried about the next step, and you're more interested in your image, position, competition, and one-upmanship than in making a contribution, the whole organization will go to work to try to block your way."[8]

One of the most effective ways to keep a rampant ego and running-away ambition in check is to put your emphasis on your boss, your colleagues, or, if you're a new manager out of graduate school, your direct reports. Making others look good (especially your boss) and helping others do their jobs will increase the impact you make and will get you positive notice.

Welcome to a New World

Young professionals leaving the insular world of academics for their full-time job may have some difficulty with this concept. Students naturally compete with each other, whether in the classroom or on the playing field. At the same time, the collegiate environment is supportive of the individual. If you want to try on an idea for size, college is the place to do it. Individual expression and deviating from the norm are not only tolerated, but also expected.

Not so in the business world, where homogeneity is valued. Certainly some business environments, such as entertainment and advertising, prize creativity and individuality. But in most cases, businesses look for employees who can fit in and help further the company's objectives. Your new employer won't want to hear how you're going to change the whole organization on the first day! The only variance from the norm that companies typically welcome is in the ability to exceed expectations (although limits exist there too).

The business world, compared with the college campus, is an alien environment. When you're in college, you are among a student cohort that is usually internationally diverse and embraces a variety of thoughts, opinions, and ideas. On the other hand, the student body tends to be around the same age.

In the business world, the international diversity may still be present, but usually on a far more limited scale. The same goes for the variance of thoughts, opinions, and ideas. On the other hand, the age range can span 30 or even 40 years. That's usually a big adjustment for young professionals, whose first job may be in a cubicle next to someone who is the same age as their parents. Your supervisor may be someone who is 10 years older than you, while your peers range from roughly the same age to 20 years older. (As you move up the ranks and become a new manager with direct reports who are older than you, it's even more of a challenge, as we'll discuss in later chapters.) Some of the people you'll meet in the work environment will have a Ph.D., and others will not have a college degree at all.

How can you work with people who have so little in common with you on the surface? The answer is simple: by taking "you" out of the equation and focusing on the common goal of accomplishing the organization's goals and objectives. In the business world, you will be measured by the work you do. That is how your boss will evaluate you and, equally important, how your peers will look at you. As a new employee it's more important that your colleagues accept you than you accept them. At the same time, they won't accept you unless you accept them.

"I am really a big believer that you have to have a whopping dose of humility at every level, in the corner office and when you first come into an organization. It goes a long way," said Andrea Jung, chairman of Avon Products. "One of the ways of demonstrating this is to show that you are committed to learning. At the same time, you need to demonstrate that you are skilled and that you are working hard. But you also have to be open to reinventing yourself all the time. Even today as CEO I have to learn new skills and take it upon myself to commit to continual self-transformation."[9]

As a new employee fresh out of college or as a new manager out of graduate school, you will have your share of challenges. Among them is to learn from a diverse group of colleagues. Some will be less educated than you but will know far more than you.

The most dramatic examples are ROTC (Reserve Officers' Training Corps) students. Upon graduation, they enter the military as officers, even though they are younger and have less experience in uniform than many others. As these young officers prepare to take charge, the most important people they have to win over are the non-commissioned officers (NCOs). They are almost always older than the ROTC-trained officers and not as well educated. But they have twice as much power because they have "local knowledge." They know how things work and how things get done.

In business, a few people usually exist who are the civilian equivalent of the NCOs, usually a long-term employee who knows everybody but never shows up on any organizational chart. But if you ask your more experienced colleagues, you'll quickly find out to whom you need to talk to get what you need or to accomplish something. It may be Marian in Human Resources or Bill in Purchasing. These are the people you need to know and whose respect you must earn.

Learning the "Local Knowledge"

In his first job as a manager out of graduate school, Warren Batts had impressive educational credentials as a Harvard MBA. But he lacked an understanding of "how things got done" at his new employer, a textile manufacturer. Left on his own by his boss to figure things out, Warren decided that the best way to learn was to ask everybody he met. "The first thing I did was to go around and interview people," Warren recalled. "I asked the simple question, 'What kind of experience have you had dealing with the mills?'"

From that interview process, he came up with a resource list of people to ask if he needed help in a particular area.

In addition, as a new manager, Warren "inherited" an assistant, a very capable woman who had been a major in the Women's Marine Auxiliary Corps and who had been with the company for many years. "A lot of my guidance came from my assistant— although it seemed at the beginning that I was her assistant! She knew all of her peers in the organization. So if we didn't have the knowledge that we needed in the corporate office, we could call one of the other plant managers who had a similar experience and make that connection."[10]

It wasn't Warren's title that won his assistant's loyalty. Rather, his respect for her, his humility, and his understanding that she knew far more about the company than he did proved what kind of individual he was. Through mutual respect, a partnership was forged that helped them both work toward accomplishing the company's goals.

While graduate students may take a job as a new manager, most undergraduates will go into the workforce as entry-level employees or trainees. It can be an abrupt shift in perspective from where you were in college. You may be coming from an environment in which you were at the top of your class or the recipient of leadership honors. But as the new employee, you'll be the trainee. If you walk around with your degree on your sleeve, you'll surely be miserable in your new environment. You won't do yourself any favors with your colleagues, either. If you adopt the attitude that this is an opportunity to learn how things are done in the organization, you will get to work more quickly and start making a contribution.

Jack Gray, former CEO at Hart Schaffner & Marx, has succinct advice for young professionals today. "It's so simple. You just work hard. Yes, you have to make sure that you dress the way you should; that's an important detail. But the most important thing is to convince everybody that you're not just interested in the money; you're interested in doing the job." He recalled an incident when there was a delay on the holding platform at the factory, and he asked a young manager to go investigate. "You could tell by looking at him that he thought this was beneath his dignity. That finished him," Jack added. "You have to convince people that you are a '1,000-percent' person— that you are willing to pay any normal price for success. Mostly that means having an attitude that is not about wondering whether you're going to be promoted or get a raise. It's the attitude of 'I've got a job to do.'"[11]

The willing attitude of a contributor also means leaving behind the past glories of your college days for the humbling reality of learning the ropes as a new employee. Consider the story of Jonathon who came from a prestigious East Coast family, was a Princeton undergraduate, and received his MBA. After graduation, he decided to go into retailing. His first job was for a large department store chain working in women's ready-to-wear, a very challenging department that had fast moving inventory. Jonathon knew he had a lot to learn, from purchasing to merchandising.

To succeed, Jonathon had to forget all about his lofty educational background and get down to what he had to learn to do his best on the job. Along the way, he had some interesting life lessons as well. Three weeks after he took the job, his wife called him at the store. "I'd like to speak with Jonathon So-and-So," she told the operator. The operator searched, but couldn't find his name in the company directory. Connected with the women's ready-to-wear department, Jonathon's wife spoke with two people there. Neither of them recognized Jonathon's name. Exasperated, she began to describe him. "He's about five-foot-ten, dark hair with glasses. He's new at the company. He's in the trainee department."

"Oh!" one of the store employees said. "You mean Johnny, the new kid! I'll get him."

Like Jonathon, you go from a world in which you were pursued by recruiters and recognized for your academic achievement and leadership ability to being the "new kid." This may last a year or at least several months. You'll know when this initial phase is over: when you begin to make a contribution that others can recognize and respect. (As for Jonathon, learning this lesson has paid off handsomely. He went on to enjoy a very successful career in retailing and more recently as an entrepreneur.)

Making Your "Personal Mosaic"

Focusing on making a contribution is not merely a crash course in humility. It is a lifelong philosophy. I can tell you from personal experience that, when I was Chairman and CEO of Bell & Howell, a New York Stock Exchange-traded information services company (today known as ProQuest), I focused as much on making a contribution to the organization as I did when I was starting out many years before.

Putting the company's goals first and letting your contribution speak for itself will do more for your career over the long term than any other strategy. I have made this philosophy the centerpiece of my "personal mosaic," and I invite you to do the same.

Your personal mosaic is composed of many pieces, large and small, shiny and dull, smooth and rough. All of them are valuable. From the many pieces, an image is formed, which is the composite of your life experience, both personal and professional. Each piece, or tile, that is set in place becomes a permanent fixture. It is very hard to chisel out and replace these pieces. Therefore, be highly selective in the tiles you choose. Throughout your life, you will add to this mosaic, a living work of art that reflects who you are and how you have come to understand the world around you. It is a reminder of where you have been, as well as a map to guide you where you are going.

SUCCESS SECRETS

➤ Your long-term success in your career will be rooted in the contribution you make, but it starts with hard work and may require delayed gratification.

➤ Find what you are truly passionate about, and build your life's work around it.

➤ Seek out and listen to trusted advisors to help you discern the best choices for your future.

➤ Having ambition is good; flaunting it is your downfall.

➤ Remember, no role is too small, no task is insignificant, and even the brightest graduate has much to learn from his or her new co-workers.

2

YOUR PERSONAL
PHILOSOPHY

Your personal ethics result more from the cumulative sum of incidental decisions than from carefully thought-out deliberations.

When it comes to ethics in business, you may have the image of a group of people sitting around a table, discussing a dilemma and making a decision. You may picture them pondering with angst the moral implications and consulting some tome of wisdom. The truth is ethics result from a series of incremental business decisions that are made in response to a situation, to correct a problem, or to take advantage of an opportunity. Many times these business decisions do have ethical implications. When you're in the thick of it, however, it's hard to tell where the business decision morphs into an ethical one. Often they coexist, although you may not realize it at the time.

The topic of ethics is openly and frequently discussed in business today, a direct result of the corporate scandals that have grabbed headlines over the past several years. From mission statements to employee newsletters, companies are emphasizing their ethical principles and practices. Shareholders, employees, and analysts are actively watching companies to see if their actions match their espoused values. This parallels the recruiting process, in which a prospective employee's honesty and integrity—which were always required but generally taken for granted—are now carefully scrutinized.

In today's environment, your personal ethics are more important than ever. Others will make judgments about you based on the actions you take and the decisions you make every day. Ethics is not a vague mind-set, nor can it be summed up with the overly simplistic goal of "do the right thing." Ethical behavior is the result of conscious, deliberate choices made with a full understanding of the consequences—both positive and negative—that will result.

The truth is you may make choices without thinking about the consequences. However, that doesn't mean there aren't any consequences! Your decisions, actions, and behaviors are like a scorecard written in permanent ink that tallies up, through multiple jobs and life changes, just how ethical you are.

Your ethics are the centerpiece of your personal philosophy—the values, principles, and beliefs that influence your behavior and actions. Whether or not you think about it consciously, your personal philosophy is the foundation of all your interactions with other people, including colleagues, managers and supervisors, friends and family members. It defines how others experience you.

That being said, how would you describe your personal philosophy? Have you given much thought to your values and standards, particularly when it comes to dealing with others in your professional and personal life? If you haven't done so already, now is the time. The reason is simple: If you want to make a difference at your company, if you aspire to become a manager one day, your sense of ethics—especially how you treat others—may be a determining factor.

Standards of personal responsibility, organizational behavior, and business ethics do not pertain only to top executives and corporate leaders. They must be embraced on all levels of the organization, from the entry-level employee to the CEO.

The emphasis on ethics and personal philosophy reflects the business world's "new order," in which companies must value "people before profits," commented Andrea Jung, chairman of Avon Products. "It is clearly a management requisite that there is compassion for the human condition before you worry about earnings per share." As a new employee or a young manager, how can you demonstrate that you're in sync with this "new order" of business? By showing respect for and genuine interest in others.

"Take the time to get to know people. Make an effort, particularly if you are an entry-level manager, to make people realize that you roll up your sleeves and work just like a normal person," Andrea added.[12]

Your Moral Compass

Each of us operates by a moral compass, a set of internal guidelines for acceptable actions, behaviors, and decisions. Founded in your family and ethnic culture, your personal ethics are developed over time and are continually adjusted with each subsequent decision you make. If you are not conscious of the implications of those decisions, your moral compass will be off. This makes the initial decisions, both business and personal, all the more important as you establish a baseline with integrity and conviction. If you're not sensitive to outside forces, including the influence of others who don't share your standards, you can drift.

The boundaries you establish early on are the lines that you vow never to cross. The more you affirm these boundaries, the stronger they become. Ignore them, and you may find that they are as penetrable as air. Early on your moral compass is influenced by your family, your teachers, and your friends, but ultimately you are responsible for it. While this ethical guidance system is internal, it is also clearly visible to other people with whom you interact. After all, actions, as they say, speak louder than words. A sense of ethics that you build over time becomes your "permanent record." What a powerful concept that is!

Your "Permanent Record"

I remember going into ninth grade and being told that from then on my grades would be very important because they would be part of my "permanent record." That meant whatever I achieved (or failed to achieve) would be permanently recorded and open for anyone to view. The same concept applies to your ethical decisions. The record of your actions is indelible, which amplifies the satisfaction of making right decisions.

To update the metaphor a bit, imagine you have a CD-ROM on the back of your head, with a "read only" disc that shows the details of every decision you make. Not only is that CD-ROM available to you to read (but never erase or alter), anyone else can view it. While corrective actions can be taken, apologies made, and courses reversed, nothing can erase the initial misstep across the ethical boundary. What remains is an important lesson learned.

Situations will arise when you may decide to override your baseline ethical standards. In these instances of situational ethics, your intellect or your gut feeling may tell you it's okay. The important part is discerning whether the situation calls for making an exception or sticking to your standards. If you make ethical exceptions too often, you may find yourself in trouble.

Unfortunately, we live in a society where many distinctions exist between truth and lies. Reading several recent political polls, I was surprised to learn that "mostly telling the truth" is now a category. Mostly telling the truth? One would surmise that the person was therefore telling "at least a few" lies. Is that acceptable? Or is it just a higher grade of unacceptable than total lying? If you think "mostly telling the truth" is acceptable, try using that line with your parents or your boyfriend/girlfriend. Just look them in the eye and tell them,

"When I say this, I'm mostly telling the truth." Will they believe any-thing you've said?

"I'm troubled by a society in which everything is gray, not black and white," observed John C. "Jack" Bogle, founder and former chairman of The Vanguard Group, whose mission in recent years has been reform of the mutual fund industry. "I think things cannot be moderately right or partially wrong. There are some things in life that are not negotiable."[13]

Ethics and Corporate Culture

You will be confronted over the years with many different circum-stances that will influence you. Among them will be the ethical practices of the company where you work. Are they in sync with your values? In addition, while many companies have statements of corpo-rate principles and values, are these standards truly reflected in the corporate culture and day-to-day actions? Is the way people are treated in line with these standards?

One way to find out is to ask early on in the interview process about these ethical principles and standards and how they are put into practice. Are concrete examples available? After you're hired, do you see consistency between what is said at the company and what occurs? What is the perception of your peers? As a young profes-sional, you are more likely to be changed by the company than you will change the company. Therefore, you must ensure that the com-pany you work for has the kind of ethical principles and standards you agree with and can carry out.

What happens, then, if something is said or done at a meeting that you believe goes against the grain of the company's values or your own sense of ethics? Pamela Forbes Lieberman, former president and chief executive officer of TruServ (now known as True Value Company), a cooperative principally of hardware stores, suggests call-ing that person on his or her actions and discussing it with them.

"If it's a peer, then pull them aside afterwards and ask them about it. It may just be a misunderstanding," she suggested. "If that person is outside what the company's culture represents and if it's a hindrance to your job, then go to a supervisor and discuss it."

A certified public accountant who has held a number of top executive positions, Pamela believes a good gauge for whether your own actions and behaviors are in sync with the company's ethics and values is to ask yourself, "If someone saw what I did and put it in print, how would I feel?" That's the lesson Pamela told all employees.

"I told them, 'Pretend that a reporter for the *Wall Street Journal* is with you every minute of the day, observing everything you do or say. At any point in time, this reporter might write something. If so, would you be embarrassed? Your goal is to be completely boring, because everything you do is according to the rules. Remember that reporters usually want to write about negative news. So you want to make sure your actions are right down the line,'" she explained.[14]

We all have our shortcomings. Even people with the loftiest intentions will fail when it comes to total honesty or total ethical behavior. What's most important, particularly as you begin your career, is to start with the best foundation possible. "Each person needs to have a set of values that makes sense to that person and that are roughly consonant with the mores of society. They shouldn't allow themselves to be pressured or pushed to give up those standards," observed William G. Bowen, president of The Andrew W. Mellon Foundation and former president of Princeton University. "If a person has questions or concerns in an area of ethics, they need to voice them and talk about them with colleagues and supervisors."

Discussing the issue can help clarify whether a moral issue exists or if an ethical line has been crossed. "It's important that people not invent moral boxes when they're not there, just as it's important to recognize the moral boxes when they are there," Bill added.[15]

Right and Wrong—Evaluating Ethical Scenarios

In your own life, you can reflect on decisions you've made in the past to see whether, in hindsight, ethical issues were involved that you may or may not have seen clearly at the time. Reflecting on the conscious ethical decisions you've already made will provide guidance for the dilemmas you encounter in the future. Often, it is only in hindsight that you can fully appreciate the ethical nature of what appeared at the time to be just a business decision.

As you read the following scenarios, you'll notice that none of them deals with anything illegal or immoral. Yet they involve ethical issues that had consequences just the same. At the end of the chapter, I'll explain what actions were taken at the time, and the consequences of those actions. But for now, imagine you're confronted with these same circumstances, and ask yourself what you would do.

The Assembly Line Competition

During the summer before he entered college many years ago, Ed worked as a materials handler in the warehouse for an electronics company. His job was to bring materials as needed to the production line for workers assembling televisions. Management had an idea to improve productivity. They held a competition among the four assembly lines at the plant. The team that made the most TV sets would win a prize.

The important thing to understand is that these television sets were made of thousands of parts, some very large and some very tiny, such as minute screws that would be used for a knob or chassis. These screws were so small that a three-inch-by-three-inch box might contain 10,000 screws. Normally, the assembly line would be given a few thousand of these screws as they were needed. But before the contest ensued, one assembly line asked for the entire box.

Ed, an 18-year-old stock boy, was faced with an ethical dilemma. For one thing, his friends worked on the assembly line. Moreover, his job was to dole out the screws and other parts as the lines asked for them, not to determine when they needed them. But he certainly knew why an assembly line wanted the whole box of screws: they wanted to hoard parts. Was that really good for production and inventory management? Was it fair to the other assembly line workers? What would happen if they began to hoard some other part?

Clearly the contest's incentive had negative consequences that management had not foreseen. As a stock boy, what should Ed have done? What would you have done in this circumstance?

Truth or Consequences

When she was finishing her undergraduate studies several years ago, Donna began to interview with a number of companies. The discussion, however, always came down to a crucial point: What were her thoughts about going to graduate school? In those days, most people pursued an MBA a year or two after graduation. They did not wait three or four years (or even longer), as is often the case now. Donna was, in fact, contemplating graduate school, but she also needed to get a job. When she told the truth, she immediately made herself ineligible for consideration. What could she do, then—lie about her intention to go to graduate school? She needed a job, even if she did end up going to graduate school in a year or two. What was the right thing to do? If you had something to disclose in an interview that might cost you the job, what would you do?

To Promote or Not to Promote

Larry was working as a manager at a large corporation, overseeing several supervisors who, in turn, were in charge of managing their staff. The role of a manager is to delegate both responsibility and authority; otherwise, everyone and everything gets micromanaged. One day, a supervisor who reported to Larry brought to his office a recommendation for a wage increase for a certain employee. At most good firms, dual approval was needed for wage increases, but a manager would rarely override a supervisor's recommendation unless there was good cause.

In this situation, Larry happened to know that the employee was a below-average performer. She was, however, an above-average complainer. The recommendation was for an above-average raise. What should Larry have done in that situation? Should he support the supervisor, to whom he had delegated authority and responsibility? Or should he have run the risk of undermining the supervisor's authority by acting on his own knowledge of the situation? What would you do?

Sisters of Charity

Years ago when I was at Hart Schaffner & Marx, one of our sales executives was seated on an airplane next to a religious sister. When she learned that this executive worked for a leading clothing manufacturer, she presented him a business proposition: The long black habits and veils of the Sisters of Charity were handmade in France. Would Hart Schaffner & Marx be able to make them?

Being a good salesman, he explained that if the company could make a man's sack coat, which was one of the most difficult pieces of clothing to manufacture, it could produce just about anything. He gave her his business card but didn't think much about their conversation until a few weeks later, when he received a sample habit and a letter requesting a price quote. He brought the issue to management.

Marketing and finance put their heads together and made a decision. The company really didn't need the work. In fact, we were at our seasonal peak and would have to open up another production facility if we took on the business. And yet, we didn't think it was right to just brush off the inquiry altogether. So we came up with a normal price for each habit and doubled it, hoping that it would be price-prohibitive for the Sisters of Charity.

We were wrong! Three weeks later, we received an order for several hundred habits. Now we were stuck. We were obligated to make the habits, even though we didn't have any spare production capacity. We opened another factory, which became my responsibility. With the price we were charging the Sisters of Charity, we more than made up for that investment. We made an extraordinary profit on the habits—so much that we began to feel guilty about our inflated price quote. What should we do? Refund some of the money or keep it? After all, we had quoted them a price that was obviously less than what they had been paying. Once we realized the amount of profit we were making on the habits, there was no question what we had to do. Even though the Sisters of Charity had accepted our price quote, it was clearly too high. Everyone in the organization agreed to give them a rebate. Needless to say, the Sisters of Charity were thrilled. And, from that day on the sisters said their novenas for "those nice men at Hart Schaffner & Marx."

The Customer Is Always Right...Or Not

Sue was a division president at a large company that was devising its first national promotion campaign. This was a new marketing approach for the company, which until then promoted its products regionally. With this national approach, however, the company was going to change its marketing strategy and also launch it with an ad on network television. This was a very exciting step for the company.

The second-largest customer, accounting for 4 to 5 percent of the business, was not in favor of this strategy. This customer always bought its products regionally, which allowed it to pit one supplier against another to get a better price. The customer was so upset by the promotion that the buyer called Sue directly to express his concern. He didn't mince words.

"I have a simple suggestion for you: Cancel the promotion right now. If you don't, not only will we forego buying this promotion from you, we will not buy anything from your company," he warned Sue. "And, if we're not going to buy it, we don't want our competitors to buy it." This customer would have purchased only several hundred thousand dollars of items in this promotion, but $4 million a year in total business. This was significant to Sue's business.

At this point, the national promotion had not been announced, so it would have been possible to cancel it. On the other hand, the customer's request was outright blackmail. The business impact, however, couldn't be overlooked. Is this a business decision or an ethical one? What would you do?

Meet the Parents...Or Not

Your girlfriend/boyfriend's parents are coming to town in two weeks, and they have invited you to join them for dinner at one of the best restaurants in town, a place you've read about but never could afford. You eagerly accept the invitation, wanting to make a good impression.

That same night, however, a U2 concert has been scheduled for your city. You and another friend had tried for weeks to get tickets, but the concert was sold out within hours. The day before the parents come into town, your friend scores a couple of tickets and invites you. What do you do? Make an excuse why you can't have dinner with the parents, and try to meet for lunch instead? Or do you pass on the concert, knowing your friend will easily find someone else to take your place?

As these scenarios illustrate, ethical decisions are rarely cut and dried. Even if the ethical course of action seems obvious, negative fallout can result. It's easy to talk about ethics as long as the right choice does not create any personal loss or embarrassment or hit you in the wallet. Also, the decision's immediate impact is not the only thing that must be weighed. Secondary and tertiary effects on others and the company as a whole must be taken into account as well. Identifying and assessing a decision's impact makes matters more complicated, which is why these situations are ethical dilemmas and not clear-cut issues.

A Good Look in the Mirror

Over time, ethical behavior allows you to make decisions that, in the long run, will make you feel good about yourself, your company, and your value system. Your ethics, your standards, and your personal integrity will not put you on some kind of moral pedestal, nor will they alienate you from others. On the contrary, your personal philosophy and standards should improve your interaction with others, enhance your friendships, and help you increase your personal satisfaction. Success (as discussed in Chapter 10, "The Successful Life") involves far more than just reaching a career pinnacle or attaining a certain level of wealth or prestige. Rather, success is multifaceted, encompassing personal and professional satisfaction. Without the firm foundation of a personal philosophy, any success you achieve will be hollow.

It's No Excuse

The fact that "everybody is doing it" or "this has become common practice" does not excuse unethical behavior. Nothing will knock your moral compass out of whack faster than these lame arguments.

The excuse that "everybody is doing it" is an immediate tip-off that whatever you're doing (or thinking of doing) is wrong. Think about when you were younger and you used this line with your parents. Chances are whatever "everybody was doing" was against the rules—whether it was staying out till a certain hour or going to a particular party. The minute those words came out of your mouth, you tipped your hand: You knew something was against the rules, but you were going to rationalize it.

The same goes in the business world. "Everybody is doing it" is no excuse for unethical behavior. Neither is "if we don't, the competitors will." As soon as you utter that phrase in a conversation with your boss or your colleagues, you have compromised your value system.

Personal Philosophy and Servant Leadership

While ethics is the cornerstone, other building blocks also make up your personal philosophy. One of the most important is your commitment to serve the greater good. Those who embrace this concept do not think in terms of "what can I get out of this," but rather "how can I serve." Committing to the greater good makes you truly a team player instead of a solo operator. It's the exact opposite of "being out for yourself."

Admittedly, it goes against the grain of what you might think the business world is like or what you've been told is the best way to get ahead. You may think that success can be attained only by impressing someone else, winning the race, or outdoing your competition. The problem with this thinking is that it is too narrow. You can become too focused on how you are positioned, the next step in your career strategy, or how you will score points in the next meeting. You fail to see the proverbial big picture and, more importantly, your part in it.

Putting the emphasis on the "greater good" or the "goals of the organization" is part of a concept called "servant leadership." It sounds like an oxymoron: to lead by serving. Yet to be most effective in today's companies and organizations, servant leadership is exactly the right concept to embrace. With servant leadership, you strive to make a meaningful contribution to the company or organization by helping those around you achieve more. Through this commitment to serve, you exhibit true leadership.

Robert K. Greenleaf defined servant leadership more than 25 years ago in his breakthrough book, *Servant Leadership: A Journey into the Nature of Legitimate Power & Greatness*. With servant leadership, the motivating desire is to serve. It is not a means to an end or a strategy to "look good" to others so that you can assume a leadership role more quickly. The servant-leader never stops serving, regardless of position or title. Servant leadership means being sensitive to and anticipating the needs of others, whether it's your boss, your colleagues, or your subordinates. By exhibiting this commitment to serve, the servant becomes an inspiring example to others. The servant becomes a leader. People will want to follow you.[16]

Servant leaders also do not fear sharing power with others by delegating. This is often a downfall of young managers. They are afraid that delegating responsibility is a sign of weakness, showing that they can't handle what they've been given. (This is addressed in Chapter 8, "The First Time-Manager.") The truth is you gain power by sharing power. Since you are ultimately responsible for what you delegate, you have expanded your ability to make a contribution by tapping into the efforts of those around you.

The servant leadership ideal also helps counter some of the "blind ambition" that can be the kiss of death for a young person in business. Having ambition is great. Goals and objectives are very important, but showing too much ambition is a problem, because you send the wrong signals. By focusing exclusively on the next step, promotion, or job title, you indicate dissatisfaction with what you're doing now. In essence, you're telling people that your current job is not as important in your view as the next opportunity. Why, then, would they entrust you with more responsibility?

When Ambition Gets in the Way

Mark, a former student, came to see me recently for some advice. He was very concerned that he had not been promoted in the last couple of years. He had received excellent reviews and had been given some good salary increases, but when bigger jobs had come up, he had not been considered. The corporation had gone through some downsizing, and he was certainly glad to still have his job. But that still didn't satisfy his desire to go to the next level. Adding to his frustrations was the fact his boss was not a strong leader, and he had not been able to have a satisfactory conversation with him about the situation.

Mark was obviously driven by his desire to get promoted, to the point that this ambition had become the topic of nearly every conversation and the subject of some email messages to his boss. His single-minded focus on getting promoted had become a detriment.

"Your boss knows you are ambitious; you don't have to tell him that. He knows you want a promotion. You need to pursue another angle," I advised him. "The next time you speak with your boss, don't ask him about the promotion. Ask him what more you can do for the company."

This shift would place the emphasis on his desire to make a bigger contribution and help the company reach its goals. I also suggested that he approach his boss about other areas in the company where he could be of assistance using his knowledge, and therefore be more productive for the company. Mark embraced these ideas, and immediately his conversations with his boss became more productive.

While the servant leader is committed to bringing out the best in others, he or she is not afraid to do his or her best as well, particularly if the accomplishments contribute to a higher goal. Greg Maddux of the Chicago Cubs, who has distinguished himself on the pitcher's mound for the sake of his team, shuns the spotlight. At the same time, he's not afraid of doing his best or giving his all, particularly in the service of his team.

Greg's philosophy, which reflects the teaching of servant leadership, is simply and elegantly stated. As he explained in a conversation with me, "Put yourself in a position to have success. Don't be afraid to find out how good you can be. Be prepared. Do your homework. Stay up-to-date. Don't rely on what happened five years ago and think it's going to happen today. Stay informed. Too much information is better than none. And if you can't sort it out, then don't be afraid to find someone to help you. I ask for help every day."[17]

With this attitude and his dedication to studying the game, no wonder Greg has earned the nickname of "The Professor." While this was "partly because he used to wear wire-rimmed glasses on the mound," *Sports Illustrated* noted, "Mostly, though, it was because of Maddux's uncanny baseball smarts."[18]

Treating Everyone Equally

Another important concept in your personal philosophy is how you treat people, particularly in the workplace. A valuable lesson from Jack Gray, of Hart Schaffner & Marx, is to treat everyone equally. No matter their title or rank, their level of education or lack thereof, each person should be valued and treated with the same respect.

Today, Jack exhibits the unassuming air he had when he was CEO. In those days, as now, he cared sincerely about other people, their opinions, and their right to speak openly about what was important to them. "I came up the hard way, so I always had compassion for anybody who had to work for a living. I treated everyone with respect," he explained.

Jack has demonstrated this philosophy in many ways over the years, including never acting like "the boss" by lording his authority over others. "Don't get me wrong; I was the boss, heart and soul, and

I was tough and in complete control of the company. But I always thought that everybody had the same right to stand up and speak their minds," he told me. "I think the whole company knew that if they had an idea and wanted to fight with me about it, I'd fight with them. And if they beat me in an argument, I'd listen to them and say good for you!"[19]

As part of his "democratic attitude," Jack also distributed stock options to every nonunion employee at the company. This was back in the 1960s, 20 years before PepsiCo made its mark with its "SharePower" plan, which granted options to a broad cross section of employees.[20]

On a practical level, Jack explained, treating everyone equally also makes it easier on you—and it will keep you from making an embarrassing gaffe. It can be very easy to assume that someone isn't important if he or she has an unassuming demeanor. If you differentiate in how you treat people based on their title or position (or what you assume to be their "rank"), you could inadvertently set yourself up for a fall. Also, don't let looks fool you. It's a common trap for young people in the business world to assume that the oldest one in the room is the person in charge. This is often not the case, so don't let this happen to you.

In addition, many people in business don't have impressive titles but wield a lot of influence because of their longevity at the company or their connections. Peggy Barr, professor emeritus at Northwestern University's School of Education and Social Policy and a former vice president of student affairs, recalled from her own career the importance of getting to know the support staff within an organization. "This meant the receptionist, the administrative assistant to your boss, and so forth. Any time I went to a new college or university, these were the first people I wanted to meet, because they controlled the access. They are the most powerful people in the organization, but a lot of young people today don't understand that," Peggy explained.

"The newly minted MBA or the new undergraduate with a BS degree from a prestigious school may think they're pretty hot. But they need to understand that, although they have the degree, they don't have the experience," she continued. "Others can help them immensely. For that to happen, they have to take a genuine interest in others. There are people from whom young professionals can learn a lot of the history. Most organizations have some parts that don't make sense at first. There is usually a story behind it. Talking to the people who have been there for a long time provides the answers."[21]

Your attitude of treating everyone equally also has another benefit, as Jack Gray advised me many years ago. Some day, he told me, you'll have to ask someone to do something for you. If you have treated people well, they'll be far more apt to help you.

Treating everyone equally cannot be a preemptive strategy in case you need to call in a favor; that's phony and manipulative. You can't adopt the "treat everyone equal" philosophy for a few days and then expect a payback. You must adopt this attitude without any expectation of receiving something in return. As you show respect for your associates—whether they work on the shipping dock, in the mailroom, or at the front desk—you'll be gaining their respect as well. Human nature being what it is, people prefer to help those whom they like.

Let me tell you what happens if you don't build up this goodwill in an organization. If you try to prove your superiority over those in lesser positions at the company, you'll find that the administrative assistants and mailroom clerks won't go out of their way to help you. When you show up at 5 p.m. with an envelope that needs to be sent by messenger or a package that absolutely must go out that day, you may get a perfunctory, "Yeah, I'll do it." But you can't be sure. If your project takes too much extra effort, it probably won't get done.

Contrast that with what happens when you have always treated everyone with equal respect and dignity. Then, when you show up at the shipping dock late one afternoon with a package that must be sent to a customer right away, people will go out of their way to help you. You would be told, "Don't worry. We'll take care of it," by shipping dock associates, even though they have stacks of boxes and parcels to send out. "I'd appreciate anything you can do," you tell them, and then leave the package without a second glance. Trust is a big part of respect.

Sure enough, the customer will get the package the very next day. You should always make it a habit to immediately go back to the shipping department to thank them for the extra effort. Everyone likes to be recognized for his or her efforts and to be reminded that we're all working together toward the company's success.

Clearly, the efforts of people who have a "lesser rank" or a "lower job" are vitally important to the company's behind-the-scenes operation, as Jack Bogle commented. "Spend more time with the humble people in the organization than with the higher-ups. They are the ones who do the real work of the company. If they vanished tomorrow, action would stop!" he said.

He told a humorously self-deprecating story from his own career, when he was founder and chief executive of The Vanguard Group. After a heart transplant, Jack had to be out of the office for two to three weeks at a stretch, once a year. Although he was still in touch with the office by phone and electronically, he was physically away from the company. "What happened at Vanguard? Nothing! But if the guy who runs the mailroom came in 15 minutes late, what happens? Chaos!"[22]

Your magnanimous attitude toward others is more than a virtue; it's a necessity for success in the business world. No matter what your job, you're not on your own. Your success is directly dependent on the efforts of others. Your recognition of that fact will help you make an even greater impact on others and your organization.

The Ethical Answers

To close the chapter, let's revisit the ethical dilemmas presented earlier. As you review the scenarios described, reflect on what you would
have done in similar circumstances, and then compare that with the
actual outcome.

Working as a stock boy at the electronics company, Ed knew what
was happening when the assembly line teams began asking for extra
parts. With a competition at stake, they wanted to hoard parts to gain
an advantage. Ed decided to go to his boss and explain everything,
even though he feared possible ramifications or at least some ill feelings among his friends on the assembly line. Ed's boss discussed the
situation with the assembly line supervisors, and the problem was
solved—with no fallout for Ed. At a very young age, Ed learned the
value of standing up for what he knew was right and ethical, even if
he was afraid that others would not look favorably on him.

As Donna applied for jobs, she knew that her interest in going to
graduate school was hurting her chances of getting hired. But she
also knew she couldn't lie and say she had no intention of pursuing a
master's degree. After much soul-searching, she realized that if a job
proved to be a real opportunity for the long term, she would post-
pone going to graduate school. That was the truth, and therefore she
could say that with a clean conscience to a prospective employer.
Donna was hired by a major corporation and did her best with the
job she was given. As it turned out, she did enroll full-time in graduate school a little over a year later. But she left with her employer's
blessing and continued to work there during the summers while she
was in graduate school.

Larry knew he couldn't sign off on the above-average salary
increase for the below-average employee. But instead of overruling
the supervisor's decision, he went to him and suggested that they talk
about it. Since the salary increase had not been announced to the

employee, worrying about having to rescind something that was already promised wasn't necessary. In their conversation, Larry focused on the individual's performance. He also stressed the impact that the salary increase would have on other employees in the department if they found out about it (and such things are rarely kept secret).

This is an important aspect of making ethical decisions. You must be aware of the impact, not only on the parties involved or the situation at hand, but also the secondary and tertiary effects. For example, in Larry's case, the impact of his decision went beyond the supervisor who reported to him and the individual who was being considered for a raise. Larry had to weigh the impact on the performance levels in that department and the integrity of the system for rewarding employees. As Larry considered the situation, he had to look beyond the immediate impact to the broader implications. Once the supervisor understood this as well, he quickly changed his mind about giving the employee the raise.

When her company's second-biggest customer threatened to pull all its purchases unless a national promotion was cancelled, Sue thought the buyer was bluffing. She even told her boss that, assuring him that the company wouldn't lose one dime of the customer's business. Sue was wrong. The customer didn't order anything from the company that year or for the next two years. While Sue stood by the ethics of her decision, she knew that it had a big impact on the company's profits—and on her own bonus, for that matter. While her boss was not happy about the revenue loss, he did support Sue in her decision. Three years later, the customer was back—and with more business than ever.

And as for the U2 tickets versus meeting the parents, the question really comes down to what you value most. If the relationship is important to you, show it by your ability to keep your commitments. Then there's no question what you should do: Enjoy dinner with the parents, and pass on the concert. You will probably have another chance to hear the group one day. If you pass on the dinner, you'll make a poor impression on your girlfriend/boyfriend and the parents that you won't change easily.

By the time you graduate from college, you've already had a great number of experiences that form your ethical system. The decisions you made—and, most importantly, how you feel about those decisions—are the basis of the moral compass that will guide you in the future. As you go forward, more recent decisions will have a greater impact on this "ethical database of decisions" than events of the past. And so it will continue throughout your life as you add to your personal mosaic of actions, behaviors, standards, beliefs, and ideals. The key is to be conscious of the decisions made and the actions taken. What appears to be a very simple business or personal decision could have a long-lasting and far-reaching impact.

SUCCESS SECRETS

- ➤ Your personal ethics are the sum of your actions, decisions, and behaviors.

- ➤ The permanent record of your ethics follows you from job to job and throughout your life.

- ➤ Servant leadership is superior to the "survivor" mentality.

- ➤ Treat everyone equally; you may not know who you're snubbing.

- ➤ Life is too short to work for an organization with ethics that don't agree with yours.

PART II:
FINDING YOUR PASSION

3

Your Network: It's All About "Giving," Not Just "Getting"

To get ahead, you must be a proven contributor and a skilled networker.

As you start your career, the concept of networking is synonymous with job searching. To get a job, conventional wisdom says, you must be plugged into a network that can push your résumé in front of the right eyes. Once you've landed that job, you need to keep building your network so that you can increase your visibility, create opportunities, and secure a promotion or land that next job.

Throughout your career, networking should be a living and ongoing exercise, a two-way channel of giving and getting as you connect with others. You may use a specific network for anything from introductions and advice to leads and access to experts. While networking is an effective tool, it's important to use it the right way. Otherwise, your networking will be all about *getting*, not also about *giving*.

A truly effective network is grounded in what you can do for others. In the most pragmatic terms, the importance of "networking to give" is really simple: No one will return your phone call when you ask for something unless you've done something for him or her first.

(The only possible exception is if you are a very important person.) When you do tap into your network, people will most likely respond to you in kind, based on the goodwill you've built with what you've given. Otherwise, you will probably be operating at a deficit, looking to make a withdrawal before you've made sufficient deposits of time and energy. If you do this right, your "networking account" will continue to grow a healthy balance.

Some people will argue against this concept. Why network, they say, if you can't get something immediately? The reason is simple: When you have a skill, talent, or expertise, it should be shared, particularly within your organization. When you network with the premise that you are providing value to others, you remove any political connotations. This lets others know that your offer of assistance doesn't have any strings attached, which will also help you become more comfortable with networking.

This kind of networking, however, is probably a far cry from what you're used to. Most of us are inundated with offers to network, whether in person or through an online forum. Seminars are billed as "networking" events. Social occasions that are sponsored by a club or organization are described as "networking opportunities." Even online, we receive email invitations to join a network of potential contacts, a practice that exploded during the dot-com times and continues to grow.

While it's fine to meet and connect with people with complementary skill sets or who may provide an introduction to a new opportunity, that's a limited view of networking. To build value for the long term, networking means developing a relationship with others. You connect with a variety of people because you have some value to add to their personal or professional lives, just as they have value to add to yours.

Making the Connection

For many recent college graduates, networking is second nature, rooted in email, instant messaging, and other online communication. For example, *Fast Company* recently described incoming business school students who were using secure Web portals provided by their colleges and universities to network with each other for everything from finding furniture to meeting other people. As the business schools viewed it, this type of networking was a help to the students and also provided them with skills to land a good job in the future. As the article noted, "When it comes to soliciting job offers, it helps to tap into an extensive—and networked—group of alumni. The sooner students start forging those bonds, schools realize, the more likely they are to reap the rewards."[23]

Networking should be purposeful, a deliberate and conscious attempt to make contact with others for a specific reason. That reason, of course, may vary from person to person. For some, networking is a one-way street, an attempt to get in touch with the right people for personal advancement. For others, networking is a more powerful and meaningful undertaking. Networking provides the channel to share and establish relationships for the future. Within an organization, networking fills a vital but often underutilized role by providing the means for people to share their knowledge and expertise.

Networking and the "Knowledge Deficit"

Robert E. Kelley, Ph.D., a professor at Carnegie Mellon's Graduate School of Industrial Administration who also consults with major companies, posed an interesting—and challenging—question to a group of "brain-powered workers," whose "chief asset is mind, not muscle."

"What percentage of the knowledge you need to do your job is stored in your own mind?" he explained in his book *How to Be a Star at Work*. "Or put another way: What percentage of your time do you spend reaching out to someone or something else for knowledge that is essential for you to get your job done? Do you know how much you don't know?"

That percentage has changed through the years, at first showing that people surveyed had about 75% of the knowledge they needed in their heads. Over time, that percentage dropped, and at one company it was as low as 10%. His conclusion was that many employees and companies suffer from what he called a "knowledge-deficit problem." The only way to bridge this gap, he advised, is through "knowledge networks."

Little wonder, then, that Professor Kelley places such a high value on networking. Among his nine work strategies that help distinguish star performers, networking ranks second. (Initiative ranks first.) He differentiates his brand of networking from the typical, me-centered variety that entails being "in the loop" on office gossip and socializing with others "who can help me in future job hunting." A star performer, he adds, knows that networking is "proactively developing dependable pathways to knowledge experts who can help me complete critical path tasks. When called upon, I share my knowledge with those who need it. The goal is to minimize the knowledge deficit that is inherent in every brain-powered job."[24]

Robert also says that the challenge for new employees is that they may not be aware of the knowledge gap in their departments or within their companies because they are in the early stages of the learning curve for their own jobs. But that is precisely where to start.

Robert suggests preparing a "knowledge map" of the department, including current projects, tasks that must be accomplished, and the individuals who have knowledge or expertise within specific areas. "Know what knowledge is available and who owns it," he explained. "That allows you to go to the right person when you need access to specific knowledge or expertise."

The knowledge map will also reveal the "missing pieces" of necessary knowledge or information in the department that are needed to complete specific projects or tasks. These gaps are opportunities for you to help others and become the resource expert. "When you know the missing pieces, spend some time reading about and researching these areas," he added. "Find out all you can so that you can be the resource person for others."[25]

Building and Maintaining Your Network

While Kelley's "knowledge map" will help you in your current job, another resource will be invaluable for your life and career. My former mentor, Professor Doriot, suggested we compile a handbook, which he called a "manufacturing notebook," that was a compendium of interesting and useful information, including people who had expertise in a particular area and insightful articles on a variety of topics. Furthermore, at Procter & Gamble, where I started my career, young trainees were encouraged to create and maintain a "job control book," which was much the same thing. Having a notebook, online database, or spreadsheet of people, information, and other resources that you keep up-to-date will be invaluable throughout your career.

Share What You Know

Young professionals are in an ideal position to become part of the knowledge network at their companies—even if they lack experience or expertise in the company's processes, product lines, or customer base. All it takes is a willingness to share what you know, whether it's designing a database, producing computer graphics, or organizing a project.

Let's say you put together a PowerPoint presentation at your boss's request. Because of your skill, the slides are very appealing. The graphics are sharp, and you've added some elements of animation to them. After the presentation, a colleague compliments you. What do you say in return? Do you simply say "Thanks," or do you use that comment as an opportunity to reach out?

When you position yourself as part of the knowledge network, you recognize your co-worker's comment as an invitation to share your expertise by saying, "I'll be glad to show you how I did that."

When you share your knowledge or expertise, you won't lose a competitive advantage by giving away what you know. All too often, young professionals and even more senior managers grapple with the concept that when they have a good idea or understand something that others do not, they must be careful how they share it. It's like gold to them that they must guard vigilantly. The opposite is true. Sharing knowledge, instead of hoarding it, increases its value. When you give knowledge away, it's multiplicative, allowing others to benefit and putting you in a position to gain access to what others know. The real payoff comes from the assurance that you've provided a valuable service to others, helping them improve their performance.

Moreover, as you share what you know, you strengthen and hone your own expertise. You may be bringing other people to a higher level, but you're advancing yourself as well.

The Dangers of Hoarding Knowledge

David, a high-potential young professional, was asked to take on a floundering international business that was started by his predecessor and build it up. He traveled frequently to foreign countries, working with existing customers and meeting new clients. Returning to company headquarters, he rarely gave a full report to his boss about the contacts he made or the promises he had given to customers, including the demands that this new international business would make on the factories in the U.S.

He wanted to be the clearinghouse for all information on the international business. Believing he could build his power within the company, he hoarded information and controlled access.

Admittedly, David was very successful in building the international business, but the way he went about it led to his downfall. He became a serious bottleneck that disrupted operations. Unwilling to change his ways, he was eventually fired.

When Schmoozing Falls Short

Now contrast this brand of networking with the "schmooze to get ahead" type. Networking as self-promotion has certainly been used by ambitious and me-centered individuals in business. Its impact can't be denied, and many successful professionals swear by the "it's who you know" brand of networking. However, networking that exists only for this purpose falls short of its potential to make a real difference in people's careers. Interestingly, this type of networking also does little to make these professionals more effective in their jobs and in managing others.

Fred Luthans, Ph.D., the George Holmes Distinguished Professor of Management at the University of Nebraska at Lincoln, did an extensive study of the habits of managers. Specifically, the study examined how much time these managers spent in four activity areas: communication, traditional managing, resources management, and networking, or socializing/politicking and interacting with others. Among the four activities, managers who were promoted the most spent the most time networking. Therefore, you can't ignore the fact that networking helps you get ahead.[26]

However, a balanced approach to networking is far better. It's not all altruism, either. Consider this example: You are among several internal candidates whom the boss is evaluating for a position in the department. As part of the selection process, the boss will most likely check with other people, including peers and managers in other departments with whom you've had contact. When the boss asks them for their feedback, they will probably base their comments on the contribution you've made, including your willingness to share your time and expertise. If you have only been schmoozing to get ahead, others will see that for what it is. But if you have made a sincere effort to be part of the larger team, they will notice that as well.

The bottom line: Networking is important, including for self-promotion. But some "checks and balances" are necessary to make sure your networking isn't just one-directional. Otherwise, little goodwill will be available to rely on when you need to tap into your network.

Tapping into Your Network

Just as others have turned to you for help, advice, and expertise, one day you will turn to others for assistance. That's when you will quickly find out just how much you have invested in others by what they are willing to give back to you. Even as you tap into your network, look for the next chance to repay the favor.

Here's a true story about two professionals, who I'll call Jim Smith and Phil Jones. They had gone to college together and kept in touch over the years. This personal connection turned out to be an important link in their professional lives many years later.

Jim Smith was a vice president of operations for a manufacturing company, but he wanted to branch out into a marketing role. Seeing no opportunities to do that in his current position, Jim knew he had to make a career change. Phil Jones, meanwhile, had risen through the ranks of management at a consumer products company. Over the years, Phil had told Jim that if he ever wanted to change jobs, his company would be interested in hiring him.

Jim knew there was no guarantee that Phil's company would have a position for him. After all, friends sometimes make promises about opportunities that don't pan out. When Jim called, he was pleased to learn that three opportunities were available at Phil's company. Jim interviewed with the company and took a job there. Grateful for Phil's referral, Jim told his friend never to hesitate to ask if he ever needed anything. As it turned out, Jim's chance to give back to Phil happened many years later, without Phil's even knowing about it at first.

While Jim moved up in his new company, Phil suddenly had to leave his management post in a corporate shake-up. Then one day, Jim's home phone rang. It was a former neighbor, Jean, who had relocated to the West Coast. Jean was part of an interviewing team, screening candidates for a top management position at a California company. One of the candidates, she said, was a man named Phil Jones, who had gone to the same college as Jim. Since Phil and Jim were about the same age, Jean thought perhaps they knew each other. Jim gave Phil a well-deserved reference that helped him land his new position.

The story of Jim Smith and Phil Jones doesn't end there. Four years later, while Jim was still at the consumer products company, another former neighbor, John, called him. John remembered walking to the train every day with Jim as they exchanged small talk about their jobs and lives. Now John was looking to fill a management position in his company, which required some specific knowledge, which he believed Jim had. Was Jim interested? Indeed, he was. As Jim interviewed for the position, he was asked for references. Among the names he gave was his friend, Phil Jones. Needless to say, Jim got the job. A year or so later, Jim's boss said to him, "I don't know Phil Jones, but I have to say he gave you the best reference I've ever heard from anyone."

This true story has two morals. The first is that you never know who your next best contact might be, perhaps a friend from college or a former neighbor. The second is, even as you receive help from your network, look for ways to give back. Both Jim and Phil were talented professionals and deserving of an enthusiastic recommendation. Their willingness to help each other made a difference in their respective careers.

Linking into Your Contacts

As you develop your network, know that resources are specifically set up to help you find and access the contacts you need. One example is LinkedIn.com, a Web site that is designed to help professionals look for job opportunities, seek out new clients, and advance their careers. Its "linking" tools allow people to invite others to join their networks and, like an interlocking web, access others' contacts as well.

Like all good networking tools, however, LinkedIn.com is a two-way street, enabling its users to give as well as receive. The site provides not only access to job listings, for example, but also provides a forum for professionals to offer assistance and information to each other.

Asking for Advice and Creating a Network

As a college graduate or young professional, you will likely find many people who are willing to help you, including as mentors. (See Chapter 7, "Developing Your Career.") They want to be part of your network. I can tell you that it is very gratifying, as an older, experienced professional, to have someone say, "I'd like to ask for your advice" or "I need your opinion on this." In general, people like to help because it makes them feel good about themselves. (That's the "giving" in this kind of networking.) Even the toughest manager will respond if you ask him or her for help.

If you're fortunate, you may find someone who is mentoring you in a most informal way. Gentle suggestions and positive feedback that nudge you to consider something or take a certain action are given to you in the normal course of business. Sometimes it's so subtle it's hard to notice. When you receive this kind of guidance from an influential person, take it to heart, because it's very valuable mentoring.

So how you do begin to network among your contacts, who will probably include not only your friends and people a few years ahead of you, but also those who are far more experienced? (See Chapter 4, "Finding Your Ideal Position.") One way is to seek out individuals whose professional experience includes working for several different companies. Often, they have a different perspective than someone who has spent most of his or her career at one company, as Pamela Forbes Lieberman relates.

"When I was in public accounting, I never really understood the concept of networking until I left the firm and began looking for a new position. I remember talking to partners at the firm who had spent 20 or 30 years there, and they wanted to be helpful to me, but they didn't get the concept," recalled Pamela, a certified public accountant and former president and chief executive officer of TruServ (now known as True Value Company). "Once I started talking with people who had multiple employers, it was a different story. They'd say, 'Let me introduce you to So-and-So. You can sit down and share your thoughts and goals with them and seek their input.' I found these people to be the most helpful, especially those who had been through the networking process themselves."[27]

For college students and young graduates, networking may involve your friends' parents and your parents' friends. These are adults with whom you already have a connection. (Your own parents, you will probably find, are the worst advisors on your career and professional development. Their emotional attachment gets in the way of their objectivity. And young people are more likely to listen to adults other than their parents.) Even if no one among your parents' friends or your friends' parents has a profession similar to what you want to pursue, they will probably know someone who does.

Moreover, these contacts will likely bring broad and deep experience with their industries and companies. When you set up a meeting, make sure it's in a very professional way. Arrange to meet them at their workplace, and dress for the meeting. This will allow you to see them in their professional world and to experience first-hand their business environment. This will also allow you to test yourself on how comfortable you feel in the business world, even if you're still a college student. How easily can you fit in? Can you carry on a conversation with people who are a generation older than you? And if you are invited to join them for lunch, what kind of impression do you make at the table?

Handling a Networking Lunch—Without Getting Egg on Your Face

You've called your best friend's father for some advice about the industry he works in. He invites you to visit him at the office and join him and a colleague for lunch. This is not the same as a burger with your friends.

For many students, mealtime etiquette is a problem that stems from the changes in families today, in which meals typically involve food eaten on the run. "Even students who are affiliated with one of the most sophisticated schools still have these problems," explained Peggy Barr, professor emeritus at Northwestern University's School of Education and Social Policy and former vice president of Student Affairs.

To address the problem, Northwestern sponsors a program to instruct students in social manners. "We did it because we felt that the socialization process of law and medical school students was lacking. Every intern eats on the run. They haven't eaten sitting down in ages. But when they get to interviews and they're sitting down for a meal and having polite conversation, they don't know what to do," she commented.

What began as a program for 75 students has grown into formal dinners for 200 or more students, who learn everything from navigating a complex silverware setting to knowing how to eat an artichoke. "We sometimes have to tell them things like, 'Don't chew with your mouth open.' We also explain how to talk and eat. What do you say if you don't like something? We talk about traveling overseas and encountering foods that you have not had before."[28]

Having polished table manners, the students learn, will not only help them make a good impression, but also will put them more at ease when having a networking lunch or, later in their careers, when they take a client out for a meal for the first time.

As you network—either as a college student looking for advice on what major to focus on or as a young professional investigating industries or pursuing job leads—you must reach beyond those in your immediate circle. In fact, Pamela Forbes Lieberman suggests reaching out to everyone you meet. To illustrate the point, she tells the story of a young man working at a large Chicago bank who went to get a haircut one day. As he sat in the barber's chair, he explained how he was looking for a new job but was having trouble contacting the right people in banking. A few days later, the president of a Chicago-area bank went into the same barbershop. As he sat in the chair, he complained to the barber about the difficult time he was having recruiting people.

"The barber went over to his card file, found the young banker's name and telephone number, and told the bank president, 'Why don't you give this guy a call?'" Pamela continued. "They got together and, in the end, the young man went to work at the bank."[29]

When you actively cultivate your network, you just never know who might be the link you can offer valuable assistance to, or who might lead you to the next opportunity.

SUCCESS SECRETS

➤ Networking is more about giving than getting.

➤ Actively seek out opportunities to fill the knowledge gap at your company.

➤ When tapping into your network, be clear about what you want.

➤ Networking will help you get promoted—after you perform.

➤ Open your network to everyone you know.

4

FINDING YOUR IDEAL POSITION

A young person's first boss is likely to exert the strongest influence on his or her new career.

—J. Sterling Livingston

One of the most frequently asked questions among those entering the job market for the first time is "What's the hot industry right now?"

Too many young graduates tailor their career plans to what they perceive as the most desirable industries, sectors, or companies. Where you apply should not be determined by "what's hot" or "where the jobs are." The starting point is where your interests lie and what will make you excited enough to get up in the morning and go to work every day. The ultimate test of a job is whether, after six or nine months, you still feel that initial enthusiasm. If you can hardly wait to get to work to meet that day's tasks and challenges, you're in the right position. If not, it's time to reevaluate things.

How do you find the ideal position? If you are hoping for a quick answer, you may be perplexed at this point. The good news is, with reflection and an honest self-assessment, you will know which opportunities to pursue. The main considerations in this quest are your passions, your key interests, and what you love to do.

Identifying Your Passions

The first step to finding the ideal position is to identify your passions. What have you done that really excites you? Finding your passion is the first and most important step in your job search because it is the lasting motivation. "When I look at friends of mine who are very successful today, it's not because of the skills we have, but because of our passion for the work," commented Andrea Jung, chairman of Avon Products.[30]

Even if all you've had are summer jobs—and not really important positions— you will still find some clues to what is most appealing to you. Perhaps you enjoyed working with the public or being around children. Perhaps you liked problem solving, or maybe you hated being tied to a desk. Working on a team or working alone may be appealing.

Start by describing a "good day" on your summer job. What made that day stand out? Was it a task? Working on a group project? Organizing something? Being challenged? Now think about a "bad day" and what made it a negative experience. From this feedback, you can start to figure out what appeals to you. You may like challenges that expand your abilities or repetitive tasks that build your proficiency and expertise. There's no right or wrong answer. Someone may find troubleshooting with customers to be challenging and rewarding when solutions can be found, while another may hate dealing with anyone who is upset. As you identify and analyze your personal preferences, patterns will emerge that will provide important career insights for the future. James Citrin, a senior director at executive recruiting firm Spencer Stuart, recommends that students spend three or four weeks clipping articles that "spark their interest" from a range of magazines and newspapers. Putting them in a file and looking back after a month will likely enable them to see patterns or clues as to what interests them.[31]

When I was a college student, I thought I'd like to work in research and product development. Luckily, I had a job one summer with American Hospital Supply Corp. (which was subsequently acquired by Baxter International, Inc.). Working in the product research and development department, I saw how slow and detailed the work was and how precise everything had to be. It was very frustrating for me. Thank goodness I learned a valuable lesson from that summer job and did not have to wait until I was launching my career for real.

As a student you should use every summer of your college years to get a real job. This time should be used wisely to gain both experience and insight into what career path is most appealing and suitable for you. Granted, with some summer jobs you don't do any real work. All you do is file or input data into spreadsheets. No matter. Even as an intern in the lowliest job, you have the opportunity to see how others work. Shadow someone for a few days, or ask to be invited to some of the meetings. Watch how people treat each other, and observe the decision-making process. You'll find out pretty quickly if this environment appeals to you and if you could see yourself working there, or if it's not a good fit.

Opportunities Outside the Box

As you evaluate your true passions and career choices, don't get pigeonholed by your major or area of study. You'd be surprised how adaptable your educational background can be. For example, an engineering major who enjoys working with children could teach science, mathematics, computers, or vocational training. To pursue the career opportunities that match your passion and personality, think outside the box—that is, beyond the confines of your background and expectations.

Elizabeth had majored in finance with the intention of going into banking. Her reason for pursuing that career was based largely on what was perceived to be a good opportunity, particularly for young women who were breaking into the ranks of investment banks and brokerage houses.

While she was job-hunting, it became apparent that banking was not her passion. Rather, it was what she thought she should be doing. A friend asked her, "What are your passions? What really excites you?" She quickly replied that she loved to travel, particularly in Spanish-speaking countries. She had taken Spanish in school and was fluent in the language. Another area of interest was the arts; she had helped stage several student productions.

With these two insights, the question was how she could turn her love of the Spanish language and culture and her interest in the arts into a career. One obvious choice was Spanish-language television. Elizabeth sent her résumé to several Spanish media companies and was soon hired by a large Spanish-language television network.

When Dreams and Expectations Don't Match Up

Sometimes students are absolutely clear about their passion. The problem, however, is that their dreams are in the opposite direction of what their parents think are the best choices for them. For example, Bob was in the midst of a career dilemma. Sportswriting was his passion. The work was effortless to him, and he could imagine himself doing this the rest of his life. The reality, he knew, was that good sportswriting jobs were scarce, and the competition was fierce. His parents believed his career goal was too risky.

Despite the odds against him, Bob's passion for sportswriting and his commitment to the profession could not be denied. He decided to give it another year, despite that this wasn't what his family expected. They wanted Bob to put his good education to use in a career that had less risk. He believed that if he didn't devote more time to his dream, he would probably regret it later. In the end, Bob's focus on his passion and his commitment to making it happen paid off. After nine more months of working for small, low-paying publications, he landed a job with a national sports magazine.

At times, like Bob, your true passions conflict with your expectations or others' expectations of you. How do you reconcile the fact that, for example, you always thought you'd become a lawyer, but teaching is more appealing? What happens if your true passion isn't what your parents (who may have paid for your education) want you to do? The only way to reconcile these differences is to address them head-on. It may be harder to change your own expectations than to alter those of your family. You have to go with your heart. Otherwise, you'll be sorry later on. To do that, you must first recognize your passions and then be bold enough to follow where they lead you.

"Throughout my career, I have been blessed with the best situations that I could be in," reflected Herman Cain, former chairman of Godfather's Pizza and now CEO and president of T.H.E. Inc., a business and leadership consulting firm.

For Herman, following his passions meant changing jobs. A Purdue University graduate with a master's degree in computer science, he switched mid-career from an executive-level position in technology to become an entry-level manager in the fast-food restaurant business. Looking back, Herman says the success he gained hasn't been "something that you lock up in a safety deposit box. Success is to be used, sometimes to make a bigger and broader impact."[32]

For some people, however, their passions may not align directly with their natural talents. This presents another set of challenges, when what you love to do is not something you're naturally good at. Obviously some limits exist here. If you'd love to be a professional golfer, but you're not very good at the game, this is not a realistic expectation. But what if you have a passion for a particular pursuit, even though you know you don't have enough talent to be a star performer? Follow that passion as best you can to see where it takes you. The more you do something, the better you can get at it. You may also be able to see how you can segue into a related area.

Sometimes this means being on the fringe of your dream. Consider the example of a student who was an outstanding member of his school's golf team. However, he was not close to becoming a professional golfer—unlike his roommate, Luke Donald, who did turn pro, made more than a million dollars on the tour in 2004 at age 26, and was a member of the winning Ryder Cup team. Instead, this student followed his passion for the sport into an adjacent area: designing, manufacturing, and selling high-quality golf hats and achieving early success.

While dreams and goals will motivate you, be sure that they are not so specific or narrowly focused that they end up stymieing you instead. If you are inflexible in what you pursue, you greatly reduce your chances of achieving that specific dream. As a result, you may not take the risk, or, if you do, you may be bitterly disappointed if you fail. A far better approach is to keep your dreams broadly focused so that you can move forward, pursuing opportunities as they arise.

As David E. Bell, chair of Harvard Business School's marketing department and two of its executive education programs, observed in his chapter of the book *Remember Who You Are: Life Stories That Inspire the Heart and Mind*, "As a rule, the more *specific* you are in any of your given ambitions, the more risky the idea of pursuing them becomes; as your objectives narrow, the number of potential pitfalls in pursuing them rises... Ninety-nine percent of the time, when people see a career path as too risky, it's because they're being insufficiently flexible in their goals. Many of my students hesitate to become entrepreneurs, for instance, for fear they won't become Bill Gates. By defining success only as dominating an industry and making billions, they've made the whole venture seem too improbable, and therefore hazardous, to ever begin."[33]

Start early in your college or professional career to broaden your view of how your dream might play out. Then, like Bob, the sportswriter, try to get a small taste of it, which will allow you to confirm that this is what you truly want to pursue. While the glamour is appealing, are you willing to do the required drudgery? If so, your dream is worth pursuing. If not, it's time to change your perspective and consider something else.

Weighing the Choices

As young professionals evaluate their career options, it's important to look beyond the superficial prestige of some jobs, such as consulting and investment banking. Recruiters may make these jobs sound very appealing for a recent college graduate: lots of travel and the opportunity to deal with top management. What they don't tell you is that the travel will probably get pretty old after the first month. And, as a junior member of the team, your dealings with top management will be very limited. What you will have to contend with are long hours and extensive travel that will impact your personal life.

Another potential drawback of these careers is that you can't "pay your dues" when you're young and then cut back on your long hours and your traveling when you get more established. The more successful you become and the more clients want to work with you, the greater your time commitment and traveling obligations. In fact, highly successful (and extremely well-paid) consultants or investment bankers may find they are working longer hours and traveling even more than when they first joined their firms. Of course, many professionals do pursue consulting and investment banking, which can be very lucrative careers. If you do go into the field, make sure the equation balances for you in order to achieve success in both your life and your career. If you expect consulting to lead to a corporate job, there is a better way: start there in the first place even if the initial financial rewards and glamour are less.

On the other end of the spectrum, some graduates shy away from a particular field, even if it is aligned with their passions, because it pays less than other jobs or industries. Social work, teaching, and nursing, while well respected, may not be lucrative fields compared with other professions. They still offer opportunities for advancement for those who want to lead. Moreover, these fields carry an intrinsic value that cannot be discounted. I can't stress how much satisfaction you will feel when you follow your dreams into an area that is truly important to you, regardless of what other people say. If you are not happy and engaged by what you do, if you do not see the value of what you do, no amount of money can make up for it.

Narrowing Down the Choices

Once you've done the basic sleuthing into your passions and interests, you're ready to start narrowing down the choices. The business world is divided into two basic categories: products and services. Are you interested in working in an industry that produces something tangible? Or would you rather work for an organization that provides some kind of service, such as accounting, law, the arts, social work, or healthcare? If you prefer a company that makes products, the possibilities include those that produce industrial goods and those that make consumer goods. High-tech products and industrial machinery may intrigue you. Or you may find the newest food products exciting.

Different industries also have different cultures. Within an industry, variations exist from company to company, but some broad generalizations apply. Some are obvious. Law firms and banks, historically, have tended to be conservative and formal, while an Internet company can be more spontaneous—even chaotic. Advertising and retail typically are very creative and competitive, while large industrial companies may place a higher value on conformity. Do a little research by reading business magazines and trade journals, talking with recruiters, and networking with other people.

As you find out more about what it's like to work within a particular field, ask yourself: Could I fit in here? Does the industry's environment match my personality (for example, laid back or assertive) and my talents and skills? Am I better suited to a creative yet competitive environment like advertising or media, or do I like a more professional, button-down environment, such as automobile manufacturing?

Industry Snapshots

Based on my experiences and perceptions, I've come up with some snapshots of a few industries to contrast their personalities and cultures. Understanding the personality and culture of the industry in which you have an interest can help you determine whether it is a good fit for you.

- The clothing industry is informal and has a more loose organizational structure than other industries. In clothing, power comes from talent, not from titles. You can become a "star" in the clothing industry on the basis of talent, which outranks both education and seniority in importance.

- The paper industry is very button-down and professional. Position and title carry a lot of weight. Professionals in this industry are very well educated and trained. Fewer stars rocket up the ranks. People understand the pecking order, knowing time and experience are the best ways to get promoted.

- Building materials has a unique culture that reflects the power struggle that is inherent in this commodity business. At any given time, depending on market conditions, the power is in the hands of either the buyer or the seller. This makes for a macho and power-based environment, in which the professionals take on the personalities of their customers. Education is less valued in this field compared with the ability to get things done.

- Business technology values both education and personal ability. While titles do matter, stars who exhibit talent, creativity, and innovation are promoted quickly, regardless of seniority.

The personality of an industry or company is reflected in two ways (although it's certainly not limited to that). The first is the kinds of managers who get promoted and why, whether on the basis of title and experience or because of individual achievement. The second way is compensation. Compensation varies from industry to industry. But when you look at the total package—salary, benefits, and other incentives and perquisites—the variability is smaller than you'll find among the individual elements.

Looking at two extreme contrasts—commercial banking and utilities versus entertainment—you can see these concepts at work. In banking or utilities, a lot of emphasis is placed on seniority and following the rules. Because of that, the majority of compensation is paid in base salary, with smaller incentives. Banks and utilities also tend to offer more job security-related benefits, such as a rich retirement plan, which encourages valuable employees to stay with the company. In entertainment, far less money is guaranteed, and a lot more is a contingent payout based on performance. If you do well, you can make a lot of money. Investment banking is the extreme—even a CEO has very modest pay but can earn huge bonuses for performance.

Gradations exist to the personalities of various industries. Airlines tend to have lower base salaries but offer incentives such as deeply discounted travel benefits. Technology companies, particularly start-ups, offer incentives (many times stock) for performance, with less emphasis on security-related benefits such as retirement. It's not unusual for a startup or a company in the early stages of its development not to have a retirement plan. (Apple Computer didn't have one for years.)

Inflection Points

Once you've chosen your industry, what companies should you target? This is a particularly important consideration in a good job market. Finding the answer requires some research on your part, but the results will be well worth the effort. Many publications list employers in the area, often by industry, size of revenue, "best places to work," and any other number of criteria. Find out what companies or organizations are located in your area.

As you examine individual companies, look for firms that are at or near an inflection point. Imagine a simple line graph. For a period of time, the line has a gentle slope or may be nearly flat. Suddenly, for some reason, the line's angle changes significantly (preferably upward). That "break" is the inflection point (see Figure 4.1).

An inflection point could be caused by a change in CEO, an introduction of a major technology, a merger or acquisition, or a change in the buying habits of consumers. This rapid change brings about some interesting phenomena at a company. The way the company always operated during the time of predictable growth no longer applies. The team's experience is no longer as valuable during these times of change. New people, new ideas, fresh energy, and emerging talent are needed to respond to the changes in the marketplace or company conditions. As a young professional, that's an opportunity waiting to be tapped.

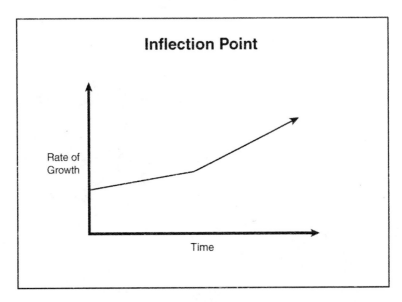

FIGURE 4.1   A company's performance over time shows a sudden break—an inflection point—that may mean an opportunity.

Negative inflection points can also be an opportunity for new talent. When the line spikes downward, the company is out of balance. To correct that balance, the company must redistribute its resources, including its people. Layoffs occur as the workforce must shrink to match the decline in product demand, output, or a change in customer habits. Even when there are massive layoffs, some people are still hired.

During my time as CEO at Bell & Howell Company in the early 1990s, we had a hiring freeze for the greater part of a year. Toward the end of the hiring freeze, we evaluated how effective this policy had been. We found that, despite the freeze, dozens of people had been hired to fill perceived needs because someone would not relocate or no internal candidate was available to retrain.

How do you find a company at an inflection point? A little due diligence—reading articles or looking through financial statements on the company's Web site—will reveal a lot about what is happening. The ideal, of course, is to anticipate an inflection point before it happens. Usually you notice it after that point has been reached, but to make the most of this opportunity, it should be as soon as possible. For example, you may read in the annual report about a new technology that the company believes has the potential to increase revenues significantly. Or it may be targeting new markets for its products that could accelerate growth. Securities analysts' reports, which are accessible online, are also a good source of information about a company and its growth prospects.

Then it's time to make contact. You may apply for a job on a company's Web site or through an Internet job-search site. Or, better yet, you may contact the company directly, expressing your interest in working there and the reasons why. Be specific in your letter. If you've always liked the candy they make, tell them. If you pass their headquarters on the highway every day, tell them. It doesn't have to be a long or even a particularly profound reason, but it does have to be true. I strongly recommend the personal touch.

Internet Versus Your Network

While many job seekers turn to the Internet, online searches may not be the most effective. A far more constructive approach is to tap into your personal and professional network (see Chapter 3, "Your Network: It's All About 'Giving,' Not Just 'Getting'). In his bestselling book *What Color Is Your Parachute? A Practical Manual for Job-Hunters and Career-Changers* (2005 Edition), author Richard N. Bolles cites research that shows a small number of jobs are found through the Internet. For example, in one study of 3,000 job seekers, only 4% landed their most recent jobs by going online. Of the remaining 96%, 40% found a job through personal referrals or by direct application.[34]

To make the most of your job-search activities, see if you know someone (or if *someone you know* knows someone!) at your target company. This is the best strategy since a good portion of job leads and information about prospective employers come from speaking with people you know. If so, ask that person for assistance in getting your résumé in front of the right people, or send it to human resources.

If you don't know anyone or can't find any other contact, you might consider writing to the CEO—although this strategy is not applicable to Fortune 100 companies. (With the very large firms, however, a higher probability exists that someone you know works there.) For other firms, consider this scenario: You are intrigued by XYZ Corp. You write to the CEO, explaining that you've always admired XYZ Corp., you've used their products for years, or that you could always picture yourself working there. You have valuable talents and skills to offer the company. Acknowledge in your letter that you know the CEO is not the right person to write to. But ask him or her to kindly pass on your résumé and letter to the appropriate department.

You probably won't get a call from the CEO's assistant. But the CEO's office generally will forward your résumé and cover letter to human resources—perhaps with a note that says, "Looks interesting" (if indeed you are interesting.) A note like that from the CEO's office will get your résumé noticed.

Résumés with a Hook—and Bait

Getting a company's attention means having a résumé that will positively reflect your talents, accomplishments, and, most importantly, the contribution you can make—in other words, looking interesting to a prospective employer. Dozens of books have been written on résumés with advice that does not need to be included or summarized here. Your focus on writing a résumé should be to ensure that it also contains certain elements that will help attract a potential employer's attention.

James Citrin, a senior director at executive recruiting firm Spencer Stuart, advises students to establish who they are quickly through the information provided. While Jim recruits top executives at leading corporations, his perspective is enlightening for college graduates and young professionals. "Here's my mental hierarchy when I read a résumé: Number 1, the name. Do I know the person? Number 2, where are they now? Do they work for a respected company? What role are they in? Next, education. Where did they go to school, and how did they do? Where did that lead them? In 20 seconds, I can get a snapshot picture of how he or she stacks up in the world."[35]

If you've done your homework, you'll know the buzzwords and phrases of the industry you're targeting. Be sure to include them in your résumé, particularly as you relate your past experience. This will not only make your résumé appealing but will also trigger keyword searches when you submit electronically. In addition to this important data, you could use a "fishing" approach. When you fish, the objective is to get the bait in front of a fish and entice it to bite. Once the fish bites the bait, it's hooked. Similarly, your résumé should be written in a way that makes it attractive to people so that they will "bite" and become hooked. One "hook" comes under a heading at the end of your résumé called "Other Data." Here, list your selected personal interests, whether it's rock climbing or watercolor portraits—the weirder the better, although it must be true.

These details prompt the question that just begs to be asked in an interview or conversation with a recruiter or potential employer. In addition, your interest in long-distance cycling, ethnic cooking, archaeology, or any other diverse topic also shows that you are a balanced, well-rounded person. If you don't have a well-developed unusual talent, but you are serious about working on one, you can note it. But be careful. If you put down "aspiring jazz musician," you can't fake it if you're not really into jazz and the person interviewing you happens to be passionate about it.

While some people believe strongly that an effective résumé must have a clear objective, I don't see this as absolutely necessary.

However, if you use an objective, it should be focused on contributing to the company's goals, not your own.

At this point you may be thinking, "But my real objective is to find a job. How can I know what contribution I'll make if I'm just starting out? Isn't it up to the company to figure out where I belong?" True, but you showcase your attitude as well as your talents and expertise in your objective. For example: "My objective is to contribute to a consumer products company through my creativity, communication skills, and interest in product marketing."

Very often students put as broad an objective as possible on their résumés, hoping to cast a wide net into the job-search waters. The problem, however, is that a generalized objective doesn't give a recruiter or someone in human resources a clear idea of where you could best serve the organization. It may also show that you aren't sure what you want to do. Recruiters want a sharply focused objective that highlights specifically how you can contribute to the company. Yes, it may eliminate some potential jobs, but most likely these would not be the ideal situation for you. By focusing your efforts, you will concentrate on a few select positions that match your passions.

Another important content area is the listing of your accomplishments. The focus should not be on what you did, but rather on the results. For example, if you had a summer job at a restaurant, what did you accomplish? Did you pick up your orders a different way that allowed you to serve more efficiently? If you worked as a file clerk in a law firm, did you find a way to improve efficiency in retrieving documents? Or did you reduce the number of misfiled or lost documents? Your accomplishments should identify the results of what you did, such as fewer errors, faster turnaround, shorter lines, more products sold. List the accomplishments using descriptive words—such as improved, faster, increased, lower cost, fewer, easier—that are followed by a noun. This is not just catchy phraseology. New online job recruiting sites have algorithms to search for these types of words.

When you submit your résumé—even if it is online through an Internet job bank or a corporate posting on a Web site—a cover letter is absolutely critical. It is the company's first exposure to you, so make it a positive one. A cover letter, written on quality paper, need not be lengthy, but it must be personalized to the company and explain why you are interested in a position there. Never send a generic or form letter to employers. Plant some "hooks" in your letter to make them want to read your résumé, such as a few of your accomplishments and why you will be a good fit for the company.

At the Interview

Volumes have also been written on handling job interviews and interviewing techniques. My intention here is to highlight some of the key elements that I believe are important for a good interview. First is preparation, which should include learning as much as you can about a company so that you can ask relevant questions. Second, rehearsing: Don't underestimate the value of rehearsing, particularly if you can find someone to videotape you. While many people shy away from this because it makes them feel awkward or embarrassed, it will provide you with valuable feedback on how you come across. The placement office at your school may offer these services, or you can ask a friend with a video recorder to do a mock interview with you.

Everyone expects you to ask questions at the interview. But it's more important to ask one really good question than to have five routine ones at your disposal. Gerry Niewoehner, a corporate psychologist and principal of Niewoehner Associates in Lake Geneva, Wis., coaches senior executives from candidacy through retirement. He believes that young professionals should ask questions of their prospective bosses and managers to discover more about the corporate culture and what management believes is important. This may be more comfortable in a second interview or plant visit, when the discussions are more serious and substantive.

"Ask the question, 'How will my performance be evaluated?' This is especially important if you are talking with your prospective new boss. Find out how you will be able to know if you are doing well, or how progress will be reviewed in a particular job," Gerry suggests.

If you are brought in for a day of interviews and meetings, capitalize on opportunities to speak with other young professionals. When you are introduced to them, look for commonalities and mutual interests that will help you make a connection.

"This usually begins with finding a common base. Perhaps you went to the same school, and you know some of the same people. Or you were both marketing majors. Whatever the common ground is, build on it," Gerry explained.

After the interview, send a handwritten note (see the Appendix, "Your Toolbox for Success"). While you may also send an email, don't think an electronic note replaces a handwritten one, which will get positive attention and could make a significant difference in whether you are called back for a second interview or ultimately offered the job.

As you make up your mind about whether to pursue this opportunity, don't overlook the value of finding people who used to work there. "Even more important is to find people who have left the company," Gerry suggests, as they will have a unique perspective.[36]

Evaluating Multiple Offers

In a good economic environment, you may have more than one job offer to weigh. So how do you choose? If your criterion is salary alone, think again. Many factors should be considered when accepting your first job, assuming that the offers you're entertaining are within the industry and companies you've targeted. Some key factors include

- Your first boss

- Corporate culture

- Desirability and affordability of the job's location

- Your interest in the work you will do (or that you will be doing very soon)

- Your compensation

I've prioritized these factors based on the typical undergraduate. For MBAs, who on average have three to four years of experience, the priorities will be different. These students, for example, have already experienced their first boss. For them, other factors become more important based on their individual experience. In addition, some situations will change the weighting of the factors. For example, geography may be the biggest consideration for you, or perhaps the type of work you want to do is most important, no matter where you have to go. That being said, let's examine each of these factors.

Your First Boss

While it may seem counterintuitive, your first boss takes top priority, because he or she will exert an inordinate influence on not only your first job but also the rest of your career. J. Sterling Livingston, a former Harvard Business School professor and founder of the Sterling Institute, a management consulting firm, stressed the importance of a young professional's first boss. In research, he found that a young person's first boss is likely to exert the strongest influence on his or her new career. He gave the example of branch managers at a West Coast bank, all of whom were in their 40s and 50s, except for one 27-year-old. "His first boss had made him a branch manager at 25 because he didn't believe it took years to become an effective manager. His talented protégé quickly excelled and trained his own assistant to assume responsibility quickly," Livingston wrote.[37]

At the other extreme, a first boss who undermines a young employee's confidence and motivation can have a lasting negative effect that is hard to shake. Some people may be able to shed any lingering doubts about their abilities after some time, while others may end up continually second-guessing themselves. As you move into your new position, make sure you have a genuine rapport with your first boss.

"Your first boss can destroy you in the organization, give you bad advice, or create such a bad impression by what he asks you to do that you have a heck of a time overcoming it," observed Warren Batts, former chairman of Premark and a member of several boards of directors.

Warren recalled a rough start with one of his bosses early in his career, when he was fresh out of graduate school. "The first week on the job, I couldn't get in to see him. But finally I managed to track him down in his office. He sat me down and said, 'Let me explain something to you: My former college roommate, the godfather of one of my children, and the half-owner of my fishing camp was fired to make room for you!' That shows the importance of knowing who is hiring you and whether or not they want you there."[38]

Luckily for Warren, his boss was essentially a fair man and a good person who did not impede his career in any way. But his boss's initial reaction showed Warren the uphill battle he was facing to develop rapport with him.

If possible, during the interview process observe how your prospective boss treats others in the department. Most people end up with a bad boss some time in their careers. But it's easier to handle a difficult manager once you have some good experiences behind you to affirm your ability and bolster your confidence.

Corporate Culture

The next factor, equal in many respects to the importance of your first boss, is corporate culture, which differs from the overall industry personality. Corporate culture includes such things as how decisions are made, the criteria by which people are promoted, how management reacts to mistakes, how successes are celebrated, how customers and shareholders are valued, and encouraging diversity and being family-friendly.

You will likely find that your boss's value system and the corporate culture are closely aligned, although occasionally you could have a bad boss in a good company. (However, you don't want to work for a good boss in a bad company, because one individual cannot sway the entire corporate culture.)

Corporate culture may be difficult to ascertain from the outside, but certainly after a few interviews at a company you should have a feel for it. Talking to others who work for the company—and, if you can, with people who used to work for the company but left—will provide insights into what it will be like working at your prospective employer.

Geographic Location

A job in Chicago will pay you $40,000 a year. A job in New York will pay you $45,000 a year. Should you take the New York job because of the extra $5,000 a year? Not without understanding the higher cost of living in New York. If you are going to relocate for a job, make sure it's to a place where you really want to live (or can afford to live). Or, if the opportunity is too great to pass up, understand the trade-off if you'll be living in a place that's less desirable.

Another geographic factor you should consider is the location of the corporate office. Perhaps you have been offered a job in a regional office based in Boston, which is one of your favorite cities.

The corporate headquarters, however, is in Phoenix, Arizona. If you rise through the company's ranks, guess where you'll end up? While you may seek other opportunities in the meantime, perhaps in Boston or elsewhere, understand that your desire (or lack thereof) to live in Phoenix will be a factor in how far you'll want to go within the company.

The Work You Will Be Doing

The next consideration is how motivated you feel about the job you will be doing, or that you will be doing shortly. Granted, some entry-level positions may seem more routine and less important because of the inevitable learning curve you will face. Still, some aspects of your job should interest you. Or you should be able to see a clear path to more tasks and responsibilities that will be challenging and make you feel that you are contributing to the greater good of the organization. If not, just having a so-so job will be very limiting, particularly as a means to showcase your talent and abilities. And don't take a job assuming that you'll be able to change the way other people work, or that someone will rescue you from your routine job as soon as he or she recognizes how bright and talented you are. If you find the workplace uninviting and the job lacking in meaning and motivation, no amount of money will make up for it.

Compensation

Salary, understandably, is a very emotional issue. All of us want to be compensated fairly, and most people aspire to a better lifestyle. Many people fail to realize, however, that compensation is actually an agreement between you and the company. The company promises to pay you "X" in exchange for your "Y" contribution. It is the basis of a healthy and mutually beneficial relationship for the future.

When it comes to your compensation, understand that almost every company has a system in place for paying people. In other words, they don't base it solely on how they feel about you. The compensation system is far more objective and complex than that. To explain, let's take look at the main components of cash compensation: base pay, incentives/bonuses, and other incentives.

Base Pay

In every organization, including the smallest companies, a system is used to determine what a job is worth. Imagine that you're starting a company. You would group certain tasks into a job and then hire someone to do that job. The smaller the company, the broader the tasks. In a larger organization, each position is more focused, with less variety of tasks but greater volume in each.

Whatever the job description, companies have developed guidelines of what the job is worth to the organization. This is also reflective of the need to pay enough to attract qualified individuals to get the job done. If a company doesn't pay enough, no one will take on the responsibilities (or, if they do, they probably won't stay very long). On the other hand, if a company pays too much, it is wasting the owners' or shareholders' money. Between these pressures of paying a fair amount and needing to get the tasks accomplished, salary targets are set.

The higher up someone is in an organization, with more responsibility and being in a position to make a greater contribution, the larger that person's salary. In addition, the higher up you go in an organization, the greater the potential variability in your pay (see Figure 4.2). As you can see, with entry-level jobs, you can quickly hit the ceiling. The only way to increase your base compensation significantly is to move to the next job category with broader responsibilities and a greater potential impact on the company's sales and profits.

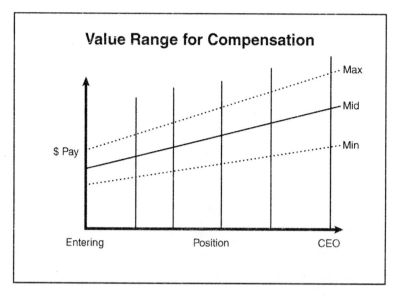

FIGURE 4.2   The greater the job responsibility, the greater the opportunity to increase your compensation.

When you have more experience, the range of what companies might pay for a particular position broadens, and you may be able to negotiate. (Be careful, however, of jumping from job to job, company to company, only to advance your pay but not your experience, knowledge, and contribution. As Professor Doriot used to say, "Don't do anything just for money.") When you are just starting out, however, pay negotiation should be the last thing you worry about. Remember, you can't negotiate your way to financial success. The only way to achieve that is to focus your energy on making a contribution to the organization instead of always looking at what's in it for you.

The "Money" Discussion

You're in discussions with a potential employer. While the opportunity looks appealing, you still have many questions about the job, what will be expected of you, and how you could grow and contribute in this position. Your prospective employer, however, wants to start the money discussion. What should you do?

Donald P. Delves, founder of The Delves Group, a Chicago-based executive compensation firm, advises professionals not to start talking about money until all the other issues are resolved. "A lot of employers will try to move you into the money discussion before you have resolved all the other issues, especially if they really want you. They use money to lure you," Don commented. "However, you would be wise to go through and address every other concern that you have first, and then talk about money. If you haven't settled all the other questions before you get into the money discussion, then you're not really serious. You're just teasing them, and they're teasing you."

Focusing too soon on money can undermine the entire job recruitment process and could prompt you to make a decision prematurely—and for the wrong reasons.

"While money is important, there are so many other aspects to an organization that you want to explore first," Don concluded. "One of them is, does it feel right? Do you like being there? The second thing is, is it challenging? If you were a good student in college, you will be frustrated in an environment where you can't learn and grow, no matter how much money you're making. You want to be part of an environment with a high level of growth opportunity. You want to work with people who know things that you want to learn and whom you respect. Are they good coaches to you? Are they people who will nurture and develop you, and tell you the hard truth when you need to hear it?"[39]

Along with your cash compensation, consider the value of all the benefits the company is offering, including vacation time, holidays, paid sick time, stock purchase plans, retirement plans, and certainly health insurance and life insurance, and possibly more. While I'm not in a position to advise people on their benefits, I will say this: If your company offers a 401(k) program, you should save enough out of each paycheck to get the full match from the company. Not only are most 401(k) plans a great way to save for the future, they also get you into the important habit as a young person of setting money aside regularly.

In addition, if you work for a large, publicly traded company, your employer may offer a stock purchase program. I suggest that you seriously consider participating in it for a couple of important reasons. First, these programs typically allow you to buy stock at a discount, which used to be the lowest share price during the quarter. Second, owning shares will allow you to feel more closely aligned with the company and with other shareholders. By having some "skin in the game," every contribution you make to the company benefits all shareholders—including yourself.

Incentives/Bonuses

A second major component of your compensation could be incentives and bonuses. Even as an entry-level employee, you may go into a job that offers potential incentives, or you may be eligible soon. Companies have different philosophies and rationale for their incentives. That is further modified by situational circumstances, some of which reflect the contribution of the individual employee. Others are based on the performance of a particular unit or division, and others are predicated on the performance of the entire company. Some companies give incentives if you simply stay with the firm. Learn how the incentive programs work, including their fundamental purpose and how you will be measured.

Bonuses and incentives are not guaranteed, nor are you automatically entitled unless you and your department or unit meet specific performance goals. Moreover, just because you receive a bonus one year doesn't mean you'll get it the next, so don't spend in anticipation of what you might receive.

Generally, if you do what's expected, you'll be rewarded with your base compensation and possibly a very modest bonus. The real payoff, however, comes from exceeding these expectations. Later in your career, bonuses for a top-level manager could skyrocket.

This reward system is unlike the world of academics where you stop with the achievement of an "A" for doing good work that meets or exceeds expectations. In the corporate world, however, you could receive a 10%–20% bonus in addition to your compensation, which is the equivalent of getting an A+. Senior people may have the opportunity to earn 100% or more of their base pay in bonuses, which is like getting an A++++! In investment banking you would probably have a comparatively low base salary but the opportunity to earn multiples of that in a bonus or as incentive compensation. To do that, however, you must measurably outperform and exceed expectations. This can be an adjustment in thinking, particularly for recent graduates who were high-achieving students.

"When you go into the business world, you graduate to another tier. You are going to be one of many top students who get hired by the company," Don Delves observed. "The goals are longer-term, more multidimensional, and complex than just getting an 'A' in school... When you are taking a class, it's relatively clearly defined how to get an 'A.' The performance measurement systems in the business world, however, are much less precise, are subject to greater error, and vary considerably by the 'grader'—much more so than at the university."[40]

Another type of bonus for which you might be eligible is the signing bonus. A signing bonus is a tool used by companies to temporarily raise the minimum that they have to offer someone to react to supply/demand imbalances in the labor market. By offering a bonus, they can increase the pay that a new employee will receive for the first year, without raising the compensation bar and skewing the whole system. Thus, signing bonuses are really about the economics of the marketplace. If you get a signing bonus, that's great. If you don't, it really doesn't mean anything in terms of your value to the organization.

Other Incentives

Typically an undergraduate is ineligible for stock option grants, the allocation of restricted shares, or other incentives. Very shortly, however, you could be eligible to receive these incentives, which offer an opportunity to build equity in the company and grow your personal assets.

Whatever your compensation package, remember it's a reward for the work you do, not an allowance for showing up. The greater the contribution you make, the more you will be valued. And the more you are valued, the greater your earning potential will be over time. Don't expect that to happen overnight. You will need to demonstrate that you have the experience and skills to handle more responsibility and make a bigger contribution.

Even though most companies have very narrow guidelines for how to pay you, particularly as a new employee, you do want to go into a job feeling that you are being treated fairly. If you receive an offer for a job that you are genuinely interested in, but the salary package is far lower than you expected, you do have some recourse. One way is to go back to the recruiter and explain that you feel a little uncomfortable with the offer: "I'd like you to assure me that the offer is fair compared with other offers the company has made." Most of the time, the recruiter will explain why and how you are being paid. Every now and then, however, the recruiter will respond that, upon reflection, the company has decided to raise your offer slightly.

A final note on salary: Keep in mind that when you compare job offers with your friends, people have a tendency to "round up." You may hear of someone getting a base salary of $55,000 a year and six weeks of vacation as an entry-level employee. But is that what they'll really be getting at the beginning? Probably not. So be careful when you're comparing job offers with others. Don't believe your new job is inadequate because of what someone else is getting (or claims to be getting). Weigh your job offer on your terms, including the big picture of long-term opportunity and a chance to get noticed by the contribution you'll be making.

SUCCESS SECRETS

➤ Follow your passion, not the "hot" industry.

➤ Don't be enamored with the superficial prestige of a job that's not right for you.

➤ Look for companies at an "inflection point."

➤ Embed "hooks" in your résumé to catch the attention of recruiters.

➤ One insightful question at the interview beats five ordinary ones.

➤ Your first boss could be the most important factor in your future success.

➤ Don't sweat your early compensation; the real payoff is over the long term.

PART III:
A SUCCESSFUL START

5

FROM DAY ONE

From Day One, your first days on the job are critical. When that time is gone, it's gone!

The day you've been waiting for has finally arrived. You're about to start a new job. All the hard work has paid off, and now you're approaching Day One as a new employee. You might be tempted to breathe the proverbial sigh of relief that the job-search process is over. The truth, however, is that you've only just begun.

Day One on your new job signals the start of the most important phase of your career. Within your first few months, you will do more to establish yourself as a good fit in the organization, as a proven contributor, and as a person of value than you probably will in the coming years. In fact, I'd go so far as to say that if you fail to get off to a strong start in the first one to three months, you will greatly undermine your chances to succeed in the company and face significant challenges to prove yourself.

The key to your success is being conscious of the fact that these early days are so important. Let's assume you have accepted an offer for a job that will begin right after graduation. Even as your friends and family congratulate you, something more pressing is on your mind: What should you concentrate on during your first 30 days on the job?

The fact that you are even asking this question proves that you've solved 90 percent of the problem.

This question reveals your acute awareness of the importance of the first impression you will make on the job and whether you will be seen as a "good fit." That depends on how well you demonstrate your commitment to making a contribution to your boss, team, department, and company.

If you are aware of this, you'll be alert and mentally prepared to make the most of these first few months. If you are not aware, however, you'll be at risk of coasting during this important time. You may be lulled into thinking that "being new" is a blanket excuse that keeps others from evaluating you too critically. Granted, many things exist that you won't know and will have to learn. Nonetheless, from Day One let your enthusiasm be your biggest contribution. Show your desire to learn as much as possible, and commit yourself to surpassing the expectations of what you can accomplish. After all, this is an exciting time in your life. You've worked hard to find the right job, so celebrate by diving into it.

An Extraordinary Career

Many young professionals enter the business world with high hopes and lofty expectations. Their dreams are as vast as the possibilities they see before them. Looking many years into the future, what does a successful career look like? Based on some very compelling research, the answer is both humbling and inspiring: Extraordinarily successful executives focus on the careers and success of others as much as—and sometimes even more than—their own careers.

That was the finding of research conducted by Spencer Stuart executive recruiters James Citrin and Richard Smith, who are also coauthors of *The 5 Patterns of Extraordinary Careers: The Guide for Achieving Success and Satisfaction*. "Extraordinarily successful executives, it turns out, were not perceived as overly self-interested. Quite the opposite was true. *Nearly 90 percent* were described as being concerned about the careers of their subordinates as much as or more than their own careers. Further, a mere 4 percent were described as being most concerned with their own careers... Our research clearly demonstrates that a leadership approach *focused on the success of others* is a truly significant pattern among successful executives."[41]

Jim Citrin brought home the point for college graduates and young professionals who want to get off to a strong start from Day One. "It's an absolute fact and it is a guaranteed success strategy, whether you're an MBA coming out of school or a CEO. If you make those around you succeed, you will be successful," Jim explained.

How, then, can a new employee, who may be in a junior or entry-level position, help others be successful? The answer is simple: Look for ways to be helpful, be willing to take on extra tasks, and be focused on the goals of your boss, your team, and your company instead of solely on your own success. This begins with a commitment to add value by exceeding expectations.

"You have to do a good job with those things that are expected of you. That's the ticket to the game," Jim added. "The average professionals think it is their job to fulfill their job objectives. Successful professionals are the ones who do what's asked of them and then over-deliver consistently, such as in sales or project management by doing more than their quota or completing something faster. But the extraordinary professionals are the ones who do what's required, but then rather than doing more of the same, they figure out what they can do that both adds value to their organization or unit and that differentiates them in the process."[42]

Admittedly, this probably won't happen overnight. As a new employee, you will have a learning curve that will be shorter or longer depending on the size of your organization, the tasks you are assigned, and how your team or department operates. Throughout this learning process, however, others will be making critical judgments about you. In a large organization, you will have more opportunities and a longer period of time, because more people will get to know you and form impressions about you. In a smaller company, the number of people with whom you interact is limited. Therefore, one or two mistakes early on will be amplified. Whatever the circumstance, expect to be "under the microscope" of your manager and co-workers.

Warren Batts, former chairman and CEO of Premark and Tupperware, observed that most people have a fair amount of tolerance for new college graduates when they are first hired. "No one expects them to come in knowing everything," he commented. "But there are those who seem to do their best, who quickly demonstrate their interpersonal skills, and who spend a good deal of time finding out how to make a contribution. That means understanding the informal system for getting things done in the organization. That desire to understand is very much appreciated in companies and will help the new employee for a long time to come."[43]

Your Success Plan from Day One

With that in mind, what should you bring with you that first day on the job? Certainly not your lunch! Seriously, from Day One you must be aware of the patterns you are establishing, including your observable behaviors, attitudes, and actions by which others will evaluate you. To do this successfully, you need a plan to get off to a strong start so that you will feel good about the company you've

chosen—just as your boss, peers, direct reports, and other colleagues
will be pleased with the company's decision to hire you.

Your Plan from Day One

- Last-minute due diligence
- Setting expectations
- Making a contribution
- Be conscious of where you spend your time
- Who are your new friends?
- Watch your work space
- Choose the right pace

The seven steps in your plan are designed to help you prepare for
your "launch date" on Day One and to carry you through the critical
first few months on the job. Let's take a look at each step individually.

Last-Minute Due Diligence

By this point in your job process, you have probably done thorough
due diligence on the company where you'll work. This includes reading information on the company's Web site, looking at analysts'
reports on the company or the industry, and speaking to people who
work for the company and/or who used to work for the company.
However, if you haven't done that yet, you had best undertake some
last-minute due diligence so that you aren't totally unprepared on
Day One.

In the days before you start working, contact your boss to see if
any material is available for you to read so that you can get up to
speed on your new job. Show that you're eager to begin making a
contribution.

Dressing for Success—the First Day

On Day One, you'll want to dress in a way that makes a good impression while being in line with your peers. You don't have to show up in a suit if the dress code is casual. In the course of your interviews, you've observed how others dress, and going along with the majority is a good idea. Just make sure you're not more casual than anyone else. Dress for success by looking the part of the new role you are assuming at the company.

What happens if you've just received your MBA and you've been hired as a new manager who must go from the front office to the factory floor? My advice is to dress in a style that won't make you look completely out of line with the factory personnel but that will also keep you in the corporate team's good graces. For example, a man may decide not to wear a tie, and a woman may opt to wear slacks instead of a skirt and jacket, in keeping with the factory environment. But you wouldn't want to show up in a T-shirt and jeans either. A good compromise would be a collared shirt and pressed trousers or slacks. Your team at the factory will view you as approachable, while your corporate peers will see you as "one of them."

Setting Expectations

As a new hire, you're probably eager to dive into the job, to see what you can do and what changes you can make. Your first concern, however, is not your own agenda. In fact, setting targets on your own can lead you astray from what you should be doing. The best approach, therefore, is to identify from Day One the boss's agenda and to make sure your efforts are focused on those priorities.

In your first few months, you probably won't accomplish much as you learn the ropes of the new job and how things are done in the organization. Nonetheless, your priority is to make sure that you are off to the right start, especially with your initial tasks and assignments. As stated earlier, based on your initiative and attitude in these early days, people will form opinions about the kind of team member you are, your diligence and commitment, and the quality of your work.

Your boss may communicate her expectations for you—including how you will work and who will train you—directly. Or she may let you know her preferences by inference. It will be up to you to pick up on your boss's signals, including who will train you.

"Does your boss want to see you in his office, or does he want you to disappear into the organization? Does he want to communicate with you through memos, or in face-to-face discussions?" asked Warren Batts. "The boss may not want you hanging around his office door all the time, and instead expects you to find out for yourself what you're supposed to do. The expectation is that you'll be trained by your peers. Other bosses may have the time, energy, and patience to invite you to come in and discuss what you're working on. This 'talking' is a subtle form of coaching, but not all bosses engage in it."[44]

Understand, too, that the flow of information from the boss may not be at the same frequency as yours. With broader responsibilities and more people to manage, your boss will likely initiate communication far less frequently. But don't go too far the other way so that you inundate your boss with updates. A good ratio is to communicate two or three times more frequently than your boss does with you (unless you have a frequent communicator as a boss, who matches you email for email.)

For that first task or project, you may very well want to overachieve. However, don't do your work at such a blistering pace that you'll have a hard time living up to the expectations that you've set for yourself. (We'll address pace later in this chapter.) In other words, plan to overachieve, but only by a measured amount. You can beat a deadline and surpass expectations of quality and content. When you go to extremes—turning in a report that was expected in two weeks after only four days—you set up expectations for yourself and your work that are unrealistic. And you could end up sending some unintended negative signals. Your peers may see you as grandstanding. Furthermore, your boss may expect you to complete every project thereafter at the same pace. If you start out working every Saturday, expect to keep that up. If you work long hours, you'll be expected to keep that up as well. Patterns are critical.

As you interact with others, let your work speak for itself. In other words, while your boss will know that you graduated with a certain grade point average or that you have an MBA, everyone else doesn't need to know that. It's much better if your co-workers get to know you through the contribution you'll make rather than your résumé. You're on a team now, so act like it! The independent style you used in college no longer fits. You will be evaluated not only on how well you do, but also how well your team performs.

Asking for "More"

Your first assignment, which you accomplished in half the expected time and with a minimum of effort, seemed a little too easy. Doesn't your boss see what you're capable of accomplishing? Perhaps you graduated with top honors, or you've just received your master's degree. You're certainly ready, willing, and able to do more. So how do you go about asking for more?

This is trickier than you might think, since you don't want to look presumptuous. And the last thing you want to convey, in words or actions, is that the job you've been hired to do is beneath you.

One way would be to tell your boss that you're eager to learn more so that you can make a greater contribution to the goals and objectives of the team, department, or company. Or you can take some initiative by taking the project you've been working on to the next level by anticipating the next steps. Don't go off on your own without your boss's agreement. But if you are hungry for more, find a way to let your boss know so that you can make a more meaningful contribution through your work.

Making a Contribution

The main purpose of your communication with your boss is to demonstrate your commitment to the company's goals and objectives and to confirm that what you're doing is in line with the boss's expectations. This is a particular challenge if your job is to work on a long-term project with few interim milestones. That's when it's up to you to establish some "mini-MBOs."

Management By Objective (MBO) is a common tool used in many businesses. Essentially, it is a set of objectives that you and your boss agree on that will guide your tasks for a period of time. You will then be managed by these objectives. Your boss may not ask you about them very often since it's presumed that your work falls in line with these objectives. In reality, however, it is very easy to get off track either because you are following your curiosity in one direction or because the project leads you on tangents.

By devising "mini-MBOs" for yourself, you set incremental objectives within the overall project or larger objective. You can then report to your boss from time to time to give periodic updates and to confirm that what you're doing is in line with the boss's expectation. What you want to avoid at all costs is finding out four months into a six-month project that you're far off target.

Warren Batts recalled from his early career working for a utility company in Georgia where he took it upon himself to come up with ways to save on engineering costs. What he didn't realize, however, was that those engineering costs were added to the company's investment, and the utility was guaranteed a fixed rate of return on the total investment. "Let's just say my efforts to save money were not appreciated," he added.[45]

Too often, young professionals resist the concept of mini-MBOs. They may think they know better than the boss, or they are so focused on making a name for themselves that they'll take any opportunity to show off what they can do—even if it's not in the best interest of their team or the project they're working on. This me-first attitude is endemic in some organizations. Ironically, it can be seen clearly in sports, where the emphasis is supposed to be on the team. Chicago Cubs pitcher Greg Maddux advises that, no matter what your job is or what you've accomplished as an individual, you can't forget who the boss is.

"You have to realize in your organization that you're working for them. You have to know who the boss is. You may be in a position one day to make your own rules, and if you get there, the more power to you. But for now, you have to roll with it," Greg explained.[46]

Young professionals may also resist mini-MBOs occasionally because they want to prove that they can handle the project themselves. They don't want to be perceived as running to the boss every five minutes to make sure they're doing okay. Believe me, periodic assessments will put you in a position of strength, not weakness. You'll be able to report on what you've done thus far and ask for clarification if results are different than you expected or if the project is taking you in a different direction.

For example, suppose a young engineer is assigned to a project to develop a new factory layout that will optimize the material flow. The engineer, however, is keenly interested in high-tech equipment. When his boss asks him how the layout project is going, he explains, "I haven't finished it yet because I'm investigating some new equipment that will change the layout." The boss replies, "No, that's not what I want. I need that layout using the equipment we already have."

Now consider the mini-MBO scenario. While working on the factory layout, the young engineer wonders if material flow could be improved if the company invested in some new high-tech equipment. At this juncture, he goes to his boss and discusses the idea. He still gets credit for showing initiative, but he doesn't run the risk of crossing boundaries and taking the project into tangential territory.

Here's another example: Recently hired by a public relations (PR) agency, a young professional is given a routine task of updating media contact lists. It's tedious to call up every magazine and newspaper and double-check the names and titles of the reporters and editors on staff. She makes a few calls every day, but sheer boredom keeps her from updating the list as quickly as possible. Instead, she spends as much time as possible with the writers at the agency, a job that keenly interests her. When her boss asks her about the list, she explains that she's made a few calls, but now she's very busy helping out with a writing project.

Now consider the mini-MBO strategy. The young PR professional completes the calls on the media list as quickly as possible and begins compiling a neatly organized list. Halfway through her calls, she notices that two publications in the area—including one she reads—are not on the list. She sends her boss a quick email to see if she should add them to the list. Her boss replies immediately that she should go ahead and thanks her for her thoroughness. When she finishes the media list, she can ask her boss for more work to broaden her knowledge of the agency.

While using mini-MBOs to gauge your progress and to keep your boss informed, you can take the initiative to tackle more work or to expand what you're doing. But don't do it on your own without your boss's knowledge. Instead, let your boss know that you'd like to volunteer for a specific task force or that you'd like to become part of a specific team, particularly if it expands your learning and your skill base. As long as your desires are expressed in the context of what you can do—as opposed to what you need to get promoted—you'll strike the necessary balance.

Mini-MBOs can also help you if you're the type of person who likes to "hide" on a work team. This problem, known as "social loafing," can be seen frequently among some college students who ride along on the momentum of everybody else's efforts to move a team project forward. Students who tend to be the laggards on the teams, however, will be at a disadvantage in the business world. The competition is tougher, and less tolerance is shown for those who don't shoulder their share of the work. If you have this tendency, you can discipline yourself through mini-MBOs by committing to your part(s) of the project and giving yourself a deadline to complete the work.

Be Conscious of Where You Spend Your Time

All of us, to some extent, are creatures of habit. That's why, when you are new on the job, you want to take extra care to vary your routine. While you will probably spend much of your time with your team or your particular department, you will want to avoid focusing all your attention there.

This takes a special awareness of where you spend your time—and where you don't. I derive this concept from "Management By Wandering Around," or MBWA (which has come to be known as Management By Walking Around). This management philosophy was embraced by Hewlett-Packard and described by Tom Peters and Robert Waterman in the classic is *In Search of Excellence: Lessons from America's Best-Run Companies*. Peters and Waterman wrote that managers at some top-performing companies such as Hewlett-Packard found that they connected better with their staffs and direct reports as they "wandered around" talking with people and learning what they were doing.[47]

If you've just received your graduate degree and you've been brought into a company as a new manager, you might want to try your own MBWA technique. But what if you've been hired as an undergraduate in an entry-level position? You're not managing anyone else. How can MBWA apply to you?

One way is to use "wandering around" to learn all you can about the company from more experienced co-workers and also to find out where your expertise and knowledge can make a contribution. Look for opportunities to fill the "knowledge gap" (see Chapter 3, "Your Network: It's All About 'Giving,' Not Just 'Getting'"), which will allow you to build your network within the company. Of course, you don't want to take this to the extreme of being a company gadfly. But if you have a chance to interact with others in another department, take advantage of this opportunity to broaden your learning. Look for ways to connect with other young professionals in the company outside of work hours, on your lunch break, or at social functions such as the company holiday party or annual picnic. Once you've made friends in other departments, you can easily stop by to visit on occasion, which will give you a chance to observe the kind of work they do and how they contribute to the company's goals.

As you establish your patterns in your new job, you need to observe where you go when you "wander around"—and where you don't. This "reverse MBWA" is a very enlightening tool to help you observe your initial patterns. What department do you rarely go to, if ever? Why is that? Is it because your day-to-day responsibilities do not take you there, or is there another reason? Do you find the work they do in that department extraneous to what you do? Do you even understand what that department does?

Furthermore, do you avoid certain people or spend little time dealing with them? Do you find yourself using the 80/20 rule, spending 80% of your time with 20% of the people? If so, you are sending a very clear signal to the other 80% of the people that you consider them to be of little interest to you, that they will not help you or coach you, and cannot teach you anything. This is a mistake as a new employee, since you may very well misjudge someone's importance in an organization, and (as you recall from Chapter 2, "Your Personal Philosophy") it's far better to treat everyone equally.

Who Are Your New Friends?

As you meet people in the company, you will probably gravitate toward some people more than others. You may, as a new, entry-level employee, form friendships with some people with whom you socialize on weekends as well. Be careful, however, as you move up the ranks not to "mix business with pleasure." In fact, as a manager you should make it a practice not to socialize with people from work. Keep strict boundaries between your personal and professional lives, because you never know who might end up reporting to you one day, or vice versa.

As a new hire, you may also find that some of your new friends at work want to capture you, inviting you to have lunch with them almost every day or monopolizing your free time. This is a trap that you must avoid. It's normal to spend 60 to 80% of your day with the same people in your department or on your team. After all, these are the co-workers with whom you interact most closely. When it comes to your free time—especially your lunch hour—make a deliberate effort to vary your patterns. Eat lunch by yourself on occasion, or with new acquaintances from outside the company (see Chapter 3). Keep in mind that someone is usually observing you and your patterns, whether it's your boss or your other team members. You don't want to be perceived as belonging to a certain clique, particularly in the first days of your new job.

Avoiding the "My" Syndrome

As you interact with people in the workplace, be careful that you don't constantly refer to people you knew in another context, whether as an undergraduate or in your previous job. This is such a common problem, you may not be aware that you're doing it. So beware! If you always mention "my school," "my classmates," or "at my university," you'll come across as parochial or even snobbish.

Your new co-workers won't care who you went to school with or what they're doing now. They'll be more interested in getting to know you and discovering what value you'll bring.

Another note of caution is not to drop names about who you know higher up in the company. Perhaps you were hired by a senior manager, or you may have a personal connection with a top executive through your family or your personal network. At work, you may be operating many tiers below this person, who could even be your boss's boss's boss! How, then, do you use this connection? The short, but emphatic, answer is: you don't.

If you let other people know that you have this connection, it will immediately work against you. It will be perceived as going over your boss's head for your own gain. Chances are the person with whom you have a connection won't appreciate it, and you certainly won't do yourself any favors.

If you know a high-ranking executive at the company, when you are at work you should do nothing to indicate that you have any connection. If you see this person socially, you should take care never to talk business. The executive will appreciate your discretion and will be impressed by how you handle yourself.

Most importantly, let your work speak for itself. Whatever opportunities come your way will be based on your ability and your proven contribution, not because someone pulled a string for you. That's not to say that your connection won't continue to work behind the scenes for you. But any endorsement you receive will be based on what you've demonstrated you can do, not merely because you know someone.

Your Work Space

Your new job may be in a cubicle or in an open, team environment. You may have an office or aspire to have one someday. No matter how big or small, the space you occupy at work is yours. This work space should reflect, to some degree, who you are. You may have pictures on your desk that are important to you, such as a photo of your boyfriend/girlfriend, an interesting place you visited, or maybe even your dog. It's okay to show your personality or to display an interest that you have, as long as it doesn't come across as garish or inappropriate for the work environment. The posters from your last concert may not be considered "appropriate art" in your new job. And, if you always had trouble keeping your bedroom at home or your apartment clean and neat, don't extend those bad habits to your work space. Adopt new habits from Day One.

Also keep in mind that, while this is your space, it's also accessible to the public. In other words, your boss, your co-workers, and potentially people from outside the company will see your work space and what it communicates about you, whether it's a passion for music or your hobby of showing dogs. But be cognizant of the message it sends and ask yourself, is this what you want people at work to know about you?

While your cubicle is a place where you can show others your personality and outside interests and even offer an appropriate glimpse into your personal life, limits exist for what is acceptable. Too much "stuff" will look messy and distracting, and anything off-color or in questionable taste is, of course, out of the question.

The Right Pace

As you settle into your new job, you will also adopt your pace of working. Is it the right pace for you and your company? As discussed earlier in the chapter, you don't want to set a pace that is twice as fast as everyone else's. You won't be able to sustain it, and others may very well resent it. Like the long-distance runner who sets a pace to win, you must find your stride.

Time management is one of the most effective means to do this. By managing your time well—keeping track of deadlines and scheduling larger tasks and projects in increments—you will be at your productive best (see the Appendix, "Your Toolbox for Success"). This means finishing projects moderately ahead of deadline, exceeding expectations for quality and content (whenever possible). If you procrastinate for a week and then stay up all night to finish a project, that's not being your productive best. Fatigue is the enemy of both productivity and accuracy.

You can't count on being able to "pull an all-nighter" to complete something, even if you're used to cramming for exams and projects at college. Understand, too, that your work habits are easily observed by others, including your boss. The last thing you want to display is erratic work habits, procrastinating for several days in a row and then staying late at the office to finish something.

Are you using your time effectively to accomplish your tasks, or are you wasting time? As my mentor, Professor Georges Doriot, used to say, you must avoid the "deadly effect of lost time." Where does time get lost? Usually it's in time-wasting activities, like spending too much time talking to others or taking too many coffee breaks. Anyone who has ever surfed the Internet knows that you can lose an hour or two online without realizing it. If you run these risks, discipline yourself with strict time management to avoid that trap.

The other trap to avoid is perfectionism, pushing deadlines to make one more effort to make something "better." A point is reached, however, when a project, report, proposal, or any other assignment is "good to go" and needs to be turned in. Spending another day—or week—on the project passes the point of diminishing returns. In time, you'll get a feel for where that point of diminishing returns is when you are preparing a project for the boss, a presentation to the board of directors, or a proposal for purchasing.

Setting the right pace also involves knowing when to keep working on a project and when to quit. Perseverance is a virtue that, like patience, is rewarded over time. Too much perseverance for the wrong reasons, however, becomes a vice. That's why it's important to know when to quit, even if your ego doesn't want you to. Let's say the project you've been working on has become bigger than life. Soon you are working on it because you love the project, not because of the results. As you become less and less objective about the project's benefits, your perseverance goes astray. You need some perspective, literally stepping back from the project and assessing where it has gone, where it's headed, and what the results have been.

If you've broken the project into "mini-MBOs" and kept your boss in the loop, it's unlikely that you'll face this problem. If you haven't done this before, however, this is the time to sit down with your boss and discuss the project's status. It could be that it's time to call it quits, even if this means that your results aren't what you had hoped. It could very well be that, no matter how many alternatives you looked at, nothing will work. That's not failure; it's accepting the reality of the situation. Without this "reality check," you could end up wasting huge amounts of time, energy, and resources on a dead-end project, when you could be investing your efforts in a new project.

When the First Few Months Are Over

The habits you demonstrate in the first few months will help establish you as a person of value and a contributor to the company's goals and objectives. Your work habits, behaviors, and attitude, taken together, will determine how people will react to you as an individual and as a co-worker. As important as this perception is, few of us ever stop to think about it.

In the Mainstream

You've landed a job in a large company. But after a few months, you realize you're outside the mainstream of the core business or the real drivers of value in the organization. For example, you may be in a division that isn't strategically critical. Or you could be a step or two removed from the line of business that gets the most focus.

In the short term, this is still a good opportunity to learn all you can and earn a reputation as a contributor and a team player. In the long term, however, this will limit your opportunities. If you hope to move on in the company, and perhaps into higher-level management one day, you will have to find a way to transfer into one of the "mission-critical" divisions.

Starting out, how do you identify the mainstream? Read the company's annual report and proxy statement, which gives the five-year history of top executives. Learn where the top managers come from. While employee newsletters may look like boilerplate, the divisions that are highlighted are worth paying attention to. Down the road, as opportunities are opened to you, this will become an important factor in determining which ones to pursue.

At the end of the first few months, you probably won't receive any external recognition. It will be a day like any other. If you've followed the plan, however, you should have received plenty of informal comments and subtle feedback from your boss on your work, your incremental progress on larger projects, and the initiative that you've shown to make sure your efforts are on track with the boss's objectives.

Some companies have a policy of providing employees with formal feedback after the first 90 days. Others are much more flexible and informal about evaluations. If you're fortunate enough to work for an organization that requires early feedback, congratulations! This is a gift to you and your career. (This is discussed further in Chapter 7, "Developing Your Career.") If not, be proactive and ask your boss for feedback in those crucial first months.

While you probably won't get any external rewards, you should feel tremendous satisfaction with yourself after these critical first few months. You will undoubtedly feel pride in what you've accomplished and knowing what you've contributed. Going forward, the positive work habits and behaviors you adopted early on will become second nature. They will be part of your work ethic and attitude and will help you become not only more successful, but also more satisfied in the job you're doing.

SUCCESS SECRETS

➤ The first 30 days on the job are more important than you may think; be prepared with a plan of action.

➤ Know your boss's agenda from Day One, and make sure your efforts are focused on those priorities.

➤ Be eager to learn more so that you can make a bigger contribution.

➤ Invite early feedback from your boss and co-workers.

6

IS GRADUATE SCHOOL RIGHT FOR YOU?

You may, of course, learn quite a bit, but in terms of career effects, the effects [of graduate school] are quite limited.

—Jeffrey Pfeffer

The MBA is worth a lot... Sure, it's not a perfect degree... But in an increasingly credential-crazed society, it definitely opens doors...

—*Business Week*

You've graduated from college, and you've taken your first job. Or, perhaps you've been in that first job for a few years. You've learned a lot about the business world and about yourself, and now you're wondering what comes next.

For many people, the answer to that question is graduate school. Full-time or part-time, days, nights, or on weekends, they attend classes toward getting a master's degree related to their field of interest. While nothing is wrong with higher education, all too often students return to college with the wrong expectations. They believe that an MBA (Master of Business Administration), or any graduate degree, for that matter, will automatically advance them on the road to success. They expect to earn more money instantly with a master's degree, particularly an MBA, without considering the investment involved or weighing what would happen if they simply pursue their career paths.

The truth is that the biggest payoffs for most master's degrees are in-depth knowledge and appreciation of the complexities and sub-tleties in your field or area of interest. In the case of an MBA, you may also gain insights into your personal style and strengths, which over time will enable you to make a bigger contribution to your company.

Some disagreement exists about what to expect from a master's degree, particularly an MBA. A graduate degree is not a necessity for having a successful and rewarding career. Granted, an advanced degree is a prerequisite in some professions, such as becoming a doc-tor, lawyer, or college professor. And, if you want to become a top executive of a company some day, an MBA from one of the "elite schools"—those ranked among the top 15 or so business schools in the country—will be extremely helpful. But a graduate degree alone won't make you into something you're not, and it isn't a guaranteed shortcut to the career of your dreams, the corner office, and a six-figure income.

I believe it's necessary to be absolutely clear on the benefit of getting an MBA and what it will and won't do for you. The fact is, while an MBA from a top school will probably draw attention to your résumé, it's not the only qualification you'll need. Your biggest asset in your pursuit of your long-term goals, both personal and profes-sional, is *you*.

"There are plenty of people out there who don't have an MBA or advanced degree, who have proven that they have the mettle, the drive, determination, and wherewithal to make a significant contribu-tion," observed Ed Wilson, associate dean emeritus of the Kellogg School of Management. "That aside, there are many people who believe, and I do too, that a young person who wants a career in management would benefit from the skills and knowledge that MBA programs provide."

If you are an intelligent and highly motivated individual and are committed to making a contribution to your company or organization, you will most likely enjoy your share of success. Furthermore, if you are that type of person, getting an advanced degree from a top school may have been part of your plan all along. It was in the back of your mind as you achieved a high grade-point average as an undergraduate and as you gained valuable work experience during your summers and when you first graduated from college. Plus, being that type of dedicated, purposeful individual, you will likely be a serious candidate for admission to a top school, assuming that you also possess good communication and interpersonal skills.

Thus, your advanced degree—in particular, an MBA—is a reflection of who you already are, not a transformation into something else. "We like to think that everybody who comes to us is already good, that they are leaving something they are already good at in order to get even better," Ed Wilson added.[48]

Graduate School: Not a "Default Decision"

Getting a graduate degree must be a purposeful endeavor, not a fallback position. "Graduate school shouldn't be the default because you don't have another plan," advised Herman Cain, CEO and president of T.H.E. Inc., a leadership and solutions company, and former chairman of Godfather's Pizza, Inc.

At the same time, college students and young professionals shouldn't agonize over the decision of whether—and when—to attend graduate school, or believe that they must make the perfect decision within the first year after receiving their undergraduate degree. The good news, particularly for those who are not sure what to do, Herman added, "is that this is not the last decision you're going to make in your career. So the first thing is to take some pressure off."

His second piece of advice is, before concentrating on the short-term goal of graduate school, look first at your long-term vision of what you might want to do with your life. "Ask yourself, what do you want to do in your wildest dreams? Then the question is do you get a job in the industry that embraces your interest, or have you chosen a field of interest that requires more graduate study immediately?" Herman observed. "Now there are those who don't have a 'wildest dream.' That's okay. Even if you don't know what your dream is, think about what you are really interested in. There are also those who say that since they were six years old they wanted to be a doctor or a pilot and so on. Even if you have that wildest dream, that doesn't mean you have an exact game plan to get there, but you are moving directionally toward that."

Interestingly, Herman's early career was not based on his "wildest dream." Rather, he took his high-school teacher's suggestion to pursue mathematics and heeded his father's advice to "get a degree where you can get a job."

"My first criteria wasn't 'Will I love it?' I didn't have that luxury," added Herman, who was raised in Atlanta and became one of the first in his family, on both sides, to graduate from college. Nonetheless, motivated by the need to pursue a career that could support him and his family, Herman was clear about why he was going to graduate school. "It became apparent after I started working that I needed a master's degree," he recalled.[49]

Although he would later make a dramatic career shift, which would take him out of technology and into the restaurant business (see Chapter 10, "The Successful Life"), Herman pursued the path that made the best sense for his career and his personal circumstances at the time.

Examining Your Motivation

The reasons for pursuing a master's degree are numerous. Often the motivation is monetary: Students believe that with an advanced degree, particularly an MBA, they will automatically earn more money. However, a master's degree provides no guarantee that your earnings power will increase. Some exceptions exist, of course. In some states, such as New York, teachers are required to have a master's degree in order to receive permanent certification. Additionally, in some professions, again such as teaching, your salary is automatically raised by a preset amount if you have a master's degree. But those are the exceptions, not the rule. Why, then, do so many students—including an estimated 100,000 graduates per year from MBA programs alone[50]—pursue a master's degree?

The pursuit of learning motivates some students. If they were business majors as undergraduates, for example, they may enroll in an MBA program to close a gap in their learning. Or they might seek an advanced degree in a field of study in which they want to be an expert. Additionally, students may pursue a master's program because they do not believe they will be competitive without an advanced degree. Another motivation is that, through graduate school, they will increase their field of contacts and the depth of their professional network.

Some people are also perennial students; they just can't make the mental shift to the business world. Others think it's better to stay in school and earn an advanced degree than to try to make it in a bad job market. We saw a few cases of this in 2000–2002, although that appears to be dwindling with the recovery in the economy. Others receive an advanced degree because of their parents' expectations. For example, students may find themselves steered toward law school by their parents even if practicing law is not their true passion. (If this is happening to you, reread Chapter 4, "Finding Your Ideal Position.")

Motivated to Make a Difference

For John, the motivation to pursue an MBA encompassed reasons that were strategic for his career—and reflected his desire to make a larger contribution to his employer.

His professional career at a Midwest manufacturer had taken him through several positions of increasing responsibility. Then, at the age of 31 and with a career goal of executive management one day, John decided to pursue an executive MBA through a weekend program. Sponsored by his employer, he was accepted into an intensive 18-month program.

"During my interview at the university, I explained that I wanted to make a difference at work. My hope is that this program will increase my leadership skills and business acumen and allow for professional networking," John explained.

He added, "My expectations after completion of this program are to develop professionally at work and continue the relationships that I have developed with several of my classmates."

The son of immigrant parents, John also had a special motivation for pursuing an MBA. He believed it was a way of "paying back" the company that had hired his father so many years ago and allowed his parents to pay for college educations for their children.

Upon reflection, many students will probably find that their motivation is a combination of several factors. At the top of their list of reasons, however, is usually the desire to increase their earnings potential. The problem, however, is that just getting your ticket punched so that you can say, "I have a master's degree," will not move you to the head of the line. In fact, it's unclear what a master's will do to improve your earnings potential in the short term.

Jeffrey Pfeffer of Stanford researched the effect of business schools on their graduates and the impact that business schools had on management practices. What he found, however, was little direct correlation between getting an MBA and landing a better-paying, more responsible job.

"...(T)he research literature is pretty clear, first of all, that unless you go to an elite school, you're probably not going to get a...much better job," he explained in a National Public Radio interview. "You may, of course, learn quite a bit, but in terms of career effects, the effects are quite limited. Even if you go to an elite school, I think evidence is very uncertain as to whether or not you're going to get a much better career. People who get into elite schools are already, of course, highly motivated, highly talented, and highly intelligent individuals, and, in many instances, they would have succeeded regardless of whether or not they wound up going to business school."[51]

Pfeffer's research illustrates the importance of native intelligence, talent, drive, and ambition. If you are born with certain attributes and develop them, you'll be a better leader, and graduate school can help you improve on the qualities you already possess. Studying with a few outstanding professors in the company of other bright and like-minded students—along with exposure to new concepts and making valuable contacts—could help you shorten the time frame to achieve the goals you probably would have attained anyway.

Given the large number of MBA programs, including full-time, part-time, and online offerings from a range of universities and institutions, students who are considering getting an advanced degree need to be discerning consumers. In other words, not all MBA degrees are created equal. An MBA from an elite school will have far more impact than a degree from a third- or fourth-tier organization. It's not just that the name—Kellogg, Harvard, Wharton, University of Chicago, Duke, Stanford—carries a certain cachet. It's because companies know that, to get into those schools, students had to meet rigorous selection criteria. An MBA from a top-tier school becomes part of your "brand."

If you are accepted into one of the top-tier graduate schools, you will heighten the benefit of getting an advanced degree—but again, as a reflection of who you are and what you have already achieved.

"With an elite school, there is a foregone conclusion that they have good professors and good students, outstanding curriculum, and good placement opportunities," Ed Wilson commented. "There is a strong relationship between the reputation of the school and the ability to attract outstanding students."[52]

Overall, those who attend an elite school may find that their investment in time, effort, tuition, and lost salary (in the case of those who quit their jobs to study full time) holds the promise of a return measured in a more successful career. In a recent feature on MBA programs and graduates, *Forbes Magazine* found that these advanced degrees do pay off in time. "Our latest survey, which measures return on investment at 85 schools, concludes that B-schools paid back quite nicely for the class of 1998—a class that worked through the boom and bust since graduation," *Forbes* stated.[53]

Pursuing a Master's

If you do decide to pursue a master's degree, there are many ways to go about it. You can leave your job to become a full-time student. Or you may decide to go part-time with a program that is offered either at night, on weekends, or in a distance learning format.

"When I was in charge of the day, night, and weekend MBA programs, I used to say to students, 'We may have three ways by which you can earn your degree. But we only give out one MBA. It doesn't say day or night or weekend program.' The value of the degree was the same in any program," Ed Wilson stated.[54]

Typically, if you go full-time, you have to quit your job and shoulder the tuition expenses yourself (although there are exceptions, which are discussed in this chapter). If you opt to go to either a night or weekend program, a large portion of the cost is usually reimbursed by your employer. For the night program, the student usually takes the initiative to apply; the company's reimbursement is typically on a course-by-course basis, providing you achieve an acceptable grade.

In the weekend programs, your company may sponsor you for admission, which makes this a joint decision.

A few real bonuses can be found in night and weekend programs. For one, you don't have to leave your job, which means you can continue on your career track, and generally the company reimbursees most of your expenses. The combination of full-time work and study is extraordinarily time-consuming and requires much discipline on your part.

MBA Programs—One Size Does Not Fit All

When Karen was applying to graduate school, she already had seven years of experience. With an undergraduate degree in accounting, Karen believed that, unless she earned an MBA, it could be an issue in her career later on. Her salary, however, had reached the point that being out of the workforce for two years to complete a full-time course of study cost $150,000, which she couldn't afford. Now add to that the cost of tuition!

Her solution was to pursue a four-quarter, full-time program. Her work experience provided her the equivalent of most of the basic courses. Thus, she was able to enroll in the summer for one quarter of courses to "fill in the blanks" of her core studies and then move into the second year of the full-time MBA program. She earned her MBA in 12 months, which minimized her lost salary, and she landed a job with a new employer after receiving her graduate degree.

If your company offers to underwrite a full-time master's program, such as an MBA, it may appear to be an offer you can't refuse! You'd be well advised, however, to consider carefully before accepting. This offer comes with strings attached. For example, when Herman Cain went to Purdue University to get his master's in computer science, he went under a scholarship from his employer at the time, the Department of the Navy. "It took me three years to qualify for it. The scholarship was based first on job performance and second upon their views of whether a person would be able to complete the program," he recalled. "They paid full salary and tuition, but in return I had to make a commitment to work an additional three years. At the time, I didn't have a problem with that." In Herman's mind, the opportunity to pursue a master's degree at a prestigious university with the tuition paid for was well worth the agreement to work an additional three years.

However, drawbacks exist to accepting such an offer from your employer. In a full-time program, you are immersed in life on cam-pus, studying and interacting with a diverse cohort of students. As part of this experience, you are exposed to many different types of companies and industries: some you study, and others you meet in recruitment situations. Once you begin looking at companies with the fresh eyes of a graduate student, your world of opportunities explodes, and your former employer will never look the same.

The probability of wanting to return enthusiastically to your employer dwindles significantly as time goes on. Yet, you have to go back. If your company sponsors you for the weekend MBA program, you will probably also be obligated—usually in writing—to stay with the company for a minimum amount of time. It's possible to escape this obligation, such as by paying back the entire cost of the tuition, but these remedies are very costly and complicated.

Another reason to go it alone is that, even after you receive your master's degree, your current employer may not view you as "pre-mium property" the way an employer in a new environment would, observed Herman Cain. "You may not be as valuable to your existing employer as you would be to the company up the street that is impressed with where you went to school and that you received this degree, perhaps while you were still working. That looks very appeal-ing to them, and they want to bring you into their environment."[55]

For these many reasons, students who want to pursue a master's degree full-time should find a way to do it on their own, even if it means quitting their jobs and taking out student loans. Later, when interview time comes and you discover the possibilities out there, you will be better off than if you are psychologically linked to your company. Leaving a job to become a full-time student is neither cheap nor easy.

The top-tier schools usually require three to four years' work experience, which in my opinion is a little too long. On the other hand, students with too little work experience will not have as much to offer class discussions. The drawback of having too much work experience is that your compensation level may have reached the point where the investment you're making to give up your day job and go back to school doesn't work. Considering the cost of school (approximately $50,000 a year) and the costs of losing your salary for two years, this can easily become a $250,000 decision.

Another option is to pursue a master's degree through a distance-learning program. A number of for-profit schools offer accredited programs, such as the University of Phoenix, DeVry University's Keller Graduate School of Management, and Cardean University (a consortium of Columbia Business School, Stanford University, the University of Chicago Graduate School of Business, Carnegie Mellon University, and the London School of Economics). Students considering a distance-learning program need to understand that having the initiative to start one of these programs is quite different from having the resolve to complete it. The dropout rates for distance-learning programs are extraordinarily high because it's up to the student to keep motivated, without peer contact. The flexibility of taking a course online—any time you want—may be appealing, but it also creates the ability to put it off.

To address this problem, the programs continue to evolve, a process that I believe will continue. In fact, distance learning for

advanced degrees will continue to grow and become more competitive with night and weekend programs. Some distance-learning programs are emulating in-class discussions by using online chats or the
exchange of emails with teaching assistants. Other programs offer
real-time lectures at local facilities that have interactive video, or they
may provide streaming video lectures that can be accessed online at
any time. And some are taking it a step further. Duke University's
Fuqua School of Business has a unique approach that combines elements of distance learning with on-site instruction in a variety of
global locations.

Whatever program option a student chooses, the educational
component should come first. The first and most important reason to
get an MBA or other master's degree is to enhance and supplement
your knowledge, whether in your professional field or a related area
of interest. Even within an MBA, which many people pursue because
of its breadth, you can still find depth in a specialty such as finance,
marketing, or operations.

Learning More About Business

When I left my job at Procter & Gamble to get my master's
degree, I was an engineer who knew very little about business.
Honestly, getting an MBA had not been my plan all along; in fact, I
hadn't seriously entertained the idea until I was a junior at
Northwestern. What confirmed my decision was the co-op experience I had as an undergraduate, spending several quarters at S.C.
Johnson and American Hospital Supply Corp. I came back from
these experiences with the conviction that, even though I had an
engineering background, I wanted to become a general manager
some day. In order for that to happen, I'd have to expand my
knowledge.

Looking back on my experience, probably one of the most valuable paybacks was the network I established through graduate
school, including friendships that have lasted 40 years. In fact, I

believe the investment of time and money in a full-time MBA program is well worth it because of the contacts that will last a lifetime.

"Payback" Through Networking

The social network that is formed through graduate school is also very rewarding. The reason these friendships formed at graduate school are so strong is because you are immersed in each other's lives. That bond extends to the spouses and partners of the full-time students because the group tends to socialize together during those years at graduate school.

You can't put a dollar value on these connections and friendships that may very well last the rest of your life. Yes, it's certainly possible that you may be able to help someone else get a job in the future, just as you may be able to tap into an opportunity through your network. However, that is not the purpose of these connections. The real value is the enrichment they bring to your life.

Job Prospects

After you receive your MBA, what are your chances of getting hired? The latest news about job prospects for MBAs is that things are getting better. Competition exists, of course, given the number of MBA graduates each year from the top schools, as well as second- and third-tier schools. In general, with economic and hiring conditions improving overall, prospects are better for MBAs getting a job after graduation—particularly if you attended one of the top schools.

While much of the focus in this chapter is on an MBA, other master's programs have varying degrees of impact on your job prospects. Again, before committing to getting an advanced degree, know your motivation for pursuing it and what you're likely to get out of this investment in money, time, and effort.

If you want to become a specialist in a particular field—for example, in a technical area such as semiconductors or satellite imaging or in rehabilitation counseling—getting a master's degree is a good idea. Through your advanced studies, you'll be able to go deeper into a specific technology or professional area. In a fairly narrow niche or specialty, companies will likely value people who have an advanced degree.

The Love of Learning

The love of learning should be a factor in every decision to pursue any master's degree. There is no guarantee that the job you'll land after receiving your master's will be any better or more lucrative than the one you left. And the job you end up with may be on par with what you would have had anyway, given your native talent and aptitude.

From an educational standpoint, what's most valuable about an MBA program is the breadth of topics you will cover. For example, you learn about operations management and the key issues that confront most companies, as well as how strategies are developed and implemented. You should also have a good understanding of business administration, organizational behavior, sales and marketing, and finance. This will help position you to become a general manager some day, although companies probably won't hire you fresh out of graduate school for that position.

While, as an MBA, you will have the broad educational experience to see the "big picture," you will still need to develop an area of expertise, such as operations or marketing or finance. You can't be a generalist; you have to establish an expertise within a narrow application or function. This will enable you to demonstrate where, and how, you can make a great contribution to your organization. Once you've done that, with your MBA credential, you will be in a better position to make a greater contribution in a broader role or elsewhere in the company.

As you start your new job out of graduate school—or you continue with the job you've had—don't walk around with "MBA" stamped on your forehead. Understand that, while you have an advanced degree, others in the workplace will have valuable knowledge and expertise to share with you. If you position yourself as someone who is willing to make a contribution to others, they will reciprocate by sharing their skills and experience—as well as their respect.

Getting into Graduate School

Once you have weighed all the factors, if you decide to pursue an advanced degree, how do you get in? After all, most graduate programs at top-tier schools are very competitive. My advice is based on my experience with business schools, but it applies to many graduate programs.

The best business schools use the case method of instruction, which includes dialogue among the students in the classes. The quality of the dialogue is a function of two things: the student's experience base and the instructor's ability to facilitate the discussion. The goal is to provide a forum and an opportunity for students to talk to each other and help instruct each other.

Because of this, top schools want to have a heterogeneous mix of backgrounds and experiences among the students, believing that this will relate directly to the quality of the dialogue and the educational experience. This is what Ed Wilson describes as an "intentional community." "We shape a class," he explained. "We like to think that every person who is admitted adds value to the program."

At Kellogg, which interviews all prospective MBA students, importance is placed on interpersonal skills and communication. Ed Wilson told of a prospective MBA student he interviewed who had strong academic qualifications but did not have good interpersonal skills. During the interview, Ed did much more of the talking than the candidate.

"We denied him, and when he came back to ask me why, I explained it was because of his interpersonal skills. I told him I would like to see him apply again in a year or two," he recalled. "He followed that advice, and he did end up enrolling a couple of years later."

Schools are also looking for leadership skills and professional experience gained in first jobs out of college, as well as in summers between semesters. Another consideration is the contribution that candidates have made to their communities or organizations in which they've been active. "Have you been a leader in an organization or just a joiner?" Ed Wilson said. "If, for example, you were president of your fraternity or sorority, did you lead it in a new direction? Did you leave it in better shape than when you came to that position?"[56]

Because the top schools are selective, they are looking for people who have proven themselves to some degree in their first jobs, including being hired by prestigious firms that are known to be very diligent in their employee screening process. Thus, if you're still an undergraduate and you're serious about getting an MBA some day, you should consider what your first job out of college will say about you. Will it give you some unique or meaningful experience in an area? It may be experience running a particular kind of project or in a specific industry. Just like the "hook" in your résumé (see Chapter 4), you will want to demonstrate how your experience makes you unique.

Now ask yourself what professional or personal experience you have that makes you unique. One student described in his application to graduate school his experiences in his first job helping build miniature submarines used to take tourists on underwater tours—which was sparked by his passion for oceanography! What in your background will help you contribute to class discussions and enrich the experience of your fellow students?

If your goal is to pursue a graduate degree, the best possible strategy is to position yourself while you are still an undergraduate. That means taking a longer-term view, knowing that the grade point average you're earning now will improve your chances of being accepted to graduate school in the future. Think of the experiences you can gain in the professional world in the next few years that will make you a desirable candidate for graduate school. One big deterrent is taking a year off after receiving your undergraduate degree and traveling in Europe. The only possible exception is if you can prove, convincingly, that your trip abroad was really to study language, art, culture, or architecture, and not just an extended vacation.

If you aren't well positioned, all is not lost. Take a look at the jobs you've had. What unique professional experiences have they provided you? For example, one of the best opportunities may be field sales. If you can demonstrate your ability in three years, you could be promoted to sales manager. In that capacity, you will likely have unique experiences within your industry and with managing others. You will also have the opportunity to learn about yourself and your personal style, which will make you a valuable participant in class discussions in graduate school.

Graduate school is not for everyone. You may enjoy a rewarding and challenging career without getting an advanced degree. And, if you do receive a master's degree, such as an MBA, you may not alter your career path, although you could potentially accelerate it a bit.

An advanced degree is an accomplishment, but one that must be viewed realistically. If you see it as a ticket to guaranteed success and instant access to a higher-level, better-paying job, you may very well be disappointed. If you want to pursue a master's degree to enhance your learning in a field of study, to fill in gaps in your educational background, and to build a broader, more in-depth network, you have a better motivation for making the investment of time and money. Most important, know that a graduate degree will not fundamentally change you or endow you with gifts and talents you don't have. What you bring to graduate school will be enhanced, but the major factor in the equation is you.

SUCCESS SECRETS

➤ Don't look for instant or guaranteed monetary rewards for getting a master's degree.

➤ Be careful of your motivation; a master's degree won't make you into something you're not.

➤ The greatest paybacks of an MBA are broadening your perspective on business and expanding your network of contacts.

➤ Enrolling in an MBA program is one thing; finishing it is quite another.

➤ Unique experiences will make you more attractive to a leading business school.

7

DEVELOPING YOUR
CAREER

**You can't negotiate your way to success. Your career
development is really about your contribution, not
your salary.**

The human resources (HR) department, you may think, is the place
you go to fill out forms, apply for a job, or find out more about benefits and programs offered by the company. While all this is true, this
department is so much more. HR, as its name implies, is truly a
resource for your career development.

At this point you may be thinking, so what? I know HR is there,
and when I need something from them, I'll go ask them. You're certainly correct. HR is the place to go for bureaucratic things like
forms, ID cards, enrolling in the company's 401(k) plan, and navigating the benefits system. HR, however, can do so much more for you.
When you understand how HR works, you can use it to your advantage for other things, like career development and coaching.

At most companies, the HR department is the facilitator for
everything from hiring to firing, promotions to layoffs, along with
administration, benefits, and compensation. A formal department
may exist only in larger companies. Nonetheless, in almost every

company someone handles HR-type functions. Even if HR is out-sourced or partially outsourced, oversight for this function is maintained internally.

You may find in your organization that the primary goal of HR is completing forms and shuffling paperwork. However, the business world continues to work to improve employee satisfaction, worker productivity, and retention by paying closer attention to the needs of employees—the human capital. While HR professionals are usually skilled at the technical side of their jobs, some also have excellent "people skills." They take a genuine interest in others, including young professionals. When you find someone like this, you have discovered a real treasure.

Finding an HR Mentor

In your career, one of the best assets you can find is an HR person who will really mentor, advise, and champion you. Starting out, having an HR person on your side can help you learn the ropes, get training you need, and eventually identify new career opportunities. When you become a manager, an experienced HR professional can be a sounding board for personnel problems, such as how to give feedback to an older employee.

I was lucky enough to work with one of best HR professionals I've ever met: Maria Rubly. She had expertise in both the technical side of the job as well as the softer, people side. Maria, who came to work for me as vice president of human resources at Bell & Howell, could handle the most complex compensation and incentive issues. At the same time, she understood human nature and always tried to provide what people really needed. Looking back at my years of work and friendship with Maria, who died as this manuscript was being completed, she exemplified the true HR professional.

Maria was also a coach to me and to others in the organization, providing help and advice on handling difficult personnel issues or communicating with the staff. If you are fortunate enough to find someone like Maria in your career, seek out this person as a coach or mentor.

Your new employer may offer a formal mentoring program that matches you up with a more senior person in the company, usually in a different department. If so, by all means take advantage of it. If not, as you look for people to mentor you, don't forget your connections in human resources. With a finger on the pulse of activity in the firm and a broad perspective on the company, HR professionals know about job openings before they are posted—even before your boss knows—and may recommend you as an internal candidate. While your boss is the main contact on your job, having HR in your corner doubles the force that's on your side.

Long before you are up for the next assignment or a promotion, HR can help you access training, seminars, courses (both internal and external), and other programs. They can help you join inter-department teams and task forces to broaden your experience and knowledge and help you connect with others. For that to happen, however, you must first establish rapport with these professionals. They must know you and understand the value you bring to the organization, as well as where your strengths and interests lie. The truth is, most people aren't in contact with HR until HR contacts them to fill out a form or sign a document. The smarter way is to get to know HR first, find out what they can do for you (after all, that's what they're there for), and what you can do for them.

Remember your networking skills. You must give long before you can get (see Chapter 3, "Your Network: It's All About 'Giving,' Not Just 'Getting'"). With HR, one of the ways to give back is to attend the events they sponsor, such as lunchtime "brown bag" programs on topics ranging from a new corporate initiative to lowering your cholesterol. Just going to these programs (which may be sparsely attended) will show them that you appreciate what they do, and you will learn something. Another way is to get involved in social programs sponsored by the company. Organizers and helpers are needed for every company picnic, holiday party, fund-raiser, and "corporate challenge" race.

As you look for additional opportunities, HR professionals can be a resource for other assignments and initiatives (although make sure your boss knows that you're working with them). Volunteer for cross-function teams, especially in the important but unglamorous areas. Working on initiatives such as waste reduction, collecting receivables, supply chain efficiency, product delivery, and billing will expand your knowledge of basic, yet highly important, aspects of the company's business. Also be on the lookout for initiatives that are sponsored by HR, such as ergonomics teams. These are great ways to learn and network.

Thomas O. Ryder, chairman and chief executive officer of The Reader's Digest Association, Inc., believes so strongly in volunteering for these unglamorous assignments that he includes them in his "Ryder's Rules for Success," which he speaks about when he addresses students. "Do the dirty jobs, the ones that no one else wants to do," Tom commented.

He recalled an incident from his own career when his boss reassigned him from the "glamorous stuff in marketing and promotion" and put him in charge of "fulfillment and bad debt."

"I hated it at the beginning. But here's the good news. My boss wanted me to go on to other things. With this experience, I learned a huge amount," Tom recalled. "If you are diligent, you can bring value to every part of the organization, and you can learn from your experiences there."[57]

Moving Vertically by Expanding Horizontally

After you have settled into your position, you will probably start wondering when you'll be promoted. That's human nature. Remember the lessons from earlier in the book: It's good to have ambition; just don't be driven by it. Before you try to push your way vertically to the next level, consider what you can accomplish by expanding horizontally. Your goal is to take on additional development jobs or assignments, which will be horizontal moves in terms of salary or grade level. Then, by increasing the areas in which you can make a contribution, you will demonstrate your value to the organization and develop a broader base from which to make an upward move. This is also where a good HR department can be of help to you.

It was not uncommon years ago for someone to have two, three, or four development jobs before being promoted. Unfortunately, many people today are impatient. What they fail to understand, however, is that with two or more development jobs, the bigger and broader the opportunities that may be available. In fact, after a few development jobs, you may have access to opportunities that would not be available to you if you followed a narrow career track composed of smaller, incremental moves upward.

You may not have to change jobs to find a development assignment. It could be a specific initiative, a seminar, or other training. It could even be an advanced degree. To find out what programs are offered through the company, contact HR. This type of development can and should occur throughout your career.

Even within your existing job, it's possible to access development opportunities. Look at the edges of your position. What other responsibilities or tasks can you pick up that will expand your scope of work and broaden your influence over and contact with other departments? At the same time, as part of your periodic updates with your boss (see Chapter 5, "From Day One"), find out how you can expand your contribution to the department, the division, or the company. Let your boss know that you're willing to take on more in order to further his or her priorities and objectives. This is contrary to what some young employees want to do. They want to finish what they have to do and get out of work, leaving early whenever they can. Your willingness to do more in order to contribute more will differentiate you.

One area that companies continue to emphasize is customer contact and satisfaction. Regardless of your role, you must be aware of how your specific responsibilities have a direct benefit to the customer. The more you can develop customer knowledge, the more effective you will be.

Learning from Customer Contact

When I was at Hart Schaffner & Marx, working in manufacturing, I was encouraged to expand my knowledge by having more direct contact with consumers. For several months, in addition to my regular job, I worked a couple of nights a week and Saturdays in a retail store, selling men's clothing.

In those days, a $150 or $200 suit was considered a big sale. The salespeople had a system of rotating who was "up" next to serve customers who came into the store. As a junior person from the factory, I was never part of the "up" system. Usually, I got the "castoff" customers that the more experienced salespeople had decided were not serious about buying, often based only on the way they looked or their first comment when they came into the store.

When I worked in one of the company's retail stores in an upscale suburban mall, however, a lot of the "castoff" customers ended up buying big-ticket items. This taught me a lot about the risk of pre-judging customers. Another important lesson was how to use time wisely. Mornings were typically slow in the retail store. You could keep busy straightening clothes on the rack or looking at new merchandise. A few of the top sales professionals, however, used this slow time to call their customers and alert them to new merchandise. The others, who were the vast majority, just sat around and talked. This was also a great observation of human nature in action, seeing who was motivated to create their own opportunities.

In my development assignment at the retail store, the payoff was far more valuable than just going through the motions so that management knew I did my time there. Most important, it was a great way to learn personal selling—selling one-on-one—which became an important skill later when I had to "sell" ideas, projects, and proposals to colleagues and upper management.

Through the experience, which was facilitated by HR, I also gained some insights into retail store operations, such as the problems of old merchandise, having ample inventory, store layouts, and merchandising ideas. In addition, the connections I made were valuable to me a few years later when I was running the company's manufacturing operations. When someone in the retail division had a problem, that person could call me directly. Or, if I needed help from someone in retail, I knew who to call. For example, in those days we used a recently developed machine that could automatically sew buttons on clothing, with the look of hand sewing. Despite our best quality control work at the factory, occasionally the machine would malfunction. My retail connections knew to call me as soon as they experienced a problem with customers returning to the store because of lost buttons. This provided a valuable early warning from the retail store, which we addressed immediately at the factory.

For my own career development, my experience at the retail store gave me valuable customer contact, something I continued throughout my career. Even when I was the top executive at Bell & Howell, I spent a day every month to six weeks going out with field salespeople to meet with customers and to learn firsthand about their needs and concerns.

New Opportunities

Just as HR plays a role in your development process, it will also be valuable as you seek out broader opportunities. Even as a new employee, you probably can't resist reading the job postings—long before you're eligible to make a move in the company. No matter. You can still read them to get a feel for the opportunities that are out there and the requirements for those jobs. Then, when you've mastered your job and expanded the contribution you can make in your current position, it's time to take the next step. If you are moving up internally, your relationship with HR will really pay off. When a department manager is looking for someone internally, HR can recommend you based on what you've done and the impact you've made at the company. When that opportunity knocks, hopefully you'll be ready.

Consider the case of Steven, who worked for two years as an assistant to the president of the company, handling many projects that put him in contact with people in other departments and divisions. One day, Steven was called into the president's office. "We need a new manager for our optical division. We think you're the person to take the job. This would mean relocating to Denver, so I want you to think about it."

Steven knew that position was open, but he never thought of himself as a candidate for it. Completely taken by surprise, he needed time to evaluate the offer and make a decision.

What did Steven need to know to make a decision? The real issue in this situation is the question that goes to the heart of the situation: "Why didn't Steven consider himself as a candidate for this opportunity?"

Steven should have known that the company had been looking to fill the manager's position for two months and, based on his skill set and experience, should have already determined whether he could be considered a candidate. Had he done that, he would have thought about the opportunity ahead of time and been prepared in case his boss made him an offer.

Performance Appraisals—More Than Just Paperwork

When you become a candidate for a new position internally, your performance will precede you. While people may know you and perhaps have worked with you, that is not the only determining factor.

Even when you are highly recommended by your boss and/or HR, a fundamental document that people will look at is your performance appraisal. Or you may be identified for a position because of the strength of your appraisal.

Although performance appraisals are a very important "track record" for your career, many people see them as nothing more than obligatory paperwork. Your boss may even grumble about having to do appraisals, particularly if he or she has a large number of direct reports. Don't see your performance appraisal as something to "get over." It's too important to your career.

Performance appraisals are collaborations between the employee and his or her boss to evaluate achievements and set objectives. Your boss will evaluate your performance, possibly including an overall grade or score. This formalized feedback, however, may be superficial or incomplete, because many bosses and managers simply aren't good at it.

"Good appraisals are an art form, and, like most great art, they're in rare supply," Tom Ryder commented. "The vast majority of people really have trouble communicating weaknesses to someone else, when in fact being clear and supportively honest is a tremendous favor that you can do for someone." Getting good feedback from your boss may be trickier than you think. It may be better to ease into the conversation than to jump right in. Tom suggests a self-appraisal, which an employee can do in conjunction with a formal appraisal or as an initiative to solicit feedback from a boss or supervisor.

"Young people could help themselves enormously, if they are not getting feedback, to submit to their boss a self-appraisal—without even asking. They would say something like, 'I thought I would do an appraisal of how I'm doing on my job and see if you agree. Are we on the same wavelength in regards to the things I do well and the things I need to work on?' That would be a tremendous icebreaker, especially if the boss is reluctant to give feedback," he observed.[58]

This strategy can be carried out by writing a short memo to your boss (assuming your boss likes written communication) that highlights your progress on projects you've been working on. As you evaluate your own job and experiences, make sure you detail the extra things you've taken on, such as additional assignments and projects. Don't dwell on routine, day-to-day tasks and responsibilities; that's what you're supposed to be doing. (However, these tasks and responsibilities must be done well.) Focus on how you have expanded your contribution, and target the areas in which you have gained additional experience.

Then ask for a few minutes to meet with your boss and discuss your memo. Once you've talked about what you're doing and confirmed that you're on target, you can approach a more personal evaluation. By starting with the quantitative—the projects you've been working on—you can establish a more comfortable atmosphere to discuss the more qualitative feedback.

Welcoming Feedback

For any professional—in particular, a new employee—it can be very difficult to accept (let alone welcome) feedback. If you're like most people, you love to hear praise, but you hate to hear criticism. That's natural. But you won't really learn if you don't hear the negative as well as the positive. If you still find this difficult, ask yourself: Would you rather not know?

It's especially important (as mentioned in Chapter 5) to get feedback early on, particularly in the first 90 days. This early dialogue and your open response to it will help build a foundation of trust between you and your manager. As you actively implement advice and corrective actions, you will not only become more effective, but you'll also show respect to the person who gave you the feedback.

Frank LaFasto, senior vice president of organization effectiveness for Cardinal Health, believes so strongly in the value of feedback that he calls it a "gift." "Feedback is the lifeblood of any organization and certainly any career. Without any opportunity to be self-corrective, we are destined to be as good as we are right now. We won't get any better," Frank explained. "Because of its importance, feedback is not something to be endured. It's something to be sought after, because that's the way that we get better. If people are only telling us about our strengths, we'll be disappointed at some point when we fall short."

Typically, feedback addresses two common shortcomings: the absence of something and the overextension of a strength. The absence of something refers to knowledge, a skill, or an understanding that a person needs in a specific area. For example, a person may have a good grasp of the overall picture but may need to understand accounting or gain a better working knowledge of the distribution channel. Overextension of a strength refers to a behavior or action that is used to the extreme. For example, someone may be results-oriented but as an overextension may focus on results to the exclusion of everyone around him or her.

If you think getting feedback is difficult, consider this. Giving it is even more difficult for most people. Why? Many people have difficulty giving feedback because it can spark conflict or an emotional response. For that reason, when you're on the receiving end of feedback, you actually are more in control than the person giving it. (That might make you feel a little better next time!)

"The most interesting thing about feedback is the receiver has far more control over the outcome than the giver," Frank added. "The giver may stumble their way through, perhaps not using the best words or the best examples. But if someone is open to feedback and wants to grow, they will pull out of the message something that helps them to get better. That's why feedback is a gift."[59]

For most young professionals, the best feedback is from a variety of sources. Number one is your boss. The second is HR. The third is a mentor or other advisor. Ideally, the fourth person is your spouse or life partner, if you are lucky enough to be with someone who truly looks out for your best interests, understands business, and is sensitive to how you come across to others. (I have been fortunate enough to be married to my trusted advisor for 45 years.) A trusted friend can also give you feedback, but usually for specific periods in your life when he or she has close contact with you. This feedback should come from someone who champions you and sees you in a different context than your colleagues.

When it comes to feedback, clearly the power rests with the receiver. To facilitate this process, Frank LaFasto offers a three-step process, which he calls the "ABCs of Feedback":

- **Attitudinal.** The first rule of receiving feedback is that it requires the appropriate frame of mind. Listen with an open mind.

- **Behavioral.** While some people prefer to give abstract comments (for example, "You could have a more positive attitude."), the person receiving the feedback should ask for concrete examples of his or her behavior. An example is "It would be helpful if you could think of a situation or example where I could have done something differently."

- **Change.** The next step is to show a willingness not just to hear the feedback, but also to act on it. Some feedback can be addressed immediately. Other development needs will require attention over time. HR could provide information about courses and training.[60]

You may also receive feedback from more experienced members of your team, particularly if your boss has delegated your training to them. Try asking them for some feedback by using a specific example. You might say, "I have a feeling I wasn't as effective as I could have been in this situation. What other techniques or approaches do you think I could use?" Or make suggestions of your own, such as, "These are the things I think I could have done better. What do you think?"

Chances are, you are receiving informal feedback constantly from those around you. Are you picking it up? It's very possible that your colleagues have been subtly trying to coach you all along. Reflect on what people have been telling you. Were the suggestions and observations you received really an attempt to give you some feedback? Do you take these opportunities to invite more constructive comments and criticism?

Additionally, many companies are instituting 360-degree appraisal systems. This concept captures input from the people who surround you and who are familiar with your work. This might include managers, supervisors, direct reports, peers, and, in a few instances, even customers and suppliers. If you're fortunate to be in a company that uses this technique, be sure to make the most of it.

Although you may not encounter 360-degree appraisals until you become a manager, some companies are utilizing them at all levels. Your manager will typically aggregate comments from several people and give you a summary of all their comments, criticisms, and suggestions. Your first response may be to try to figure out who said what. Despite that temptation, it is crucial that you relax, accept the feedback, and really learn and grow from it. After all, your team's perceptions of you are their reality. Even if you think some of the comments are undeserved, you need to address them. (By the way, as a new employee you may be asked to give 360-degree feedback on your boss. Although comments are confidential, you may be scared that your boss will figure out what you said. The best advice is to be as honest and objective as possible, but never extreme, because you're new and your frame of reference is limited.)

The actions you take after you receive feedback—your willingness to listen, absorb it, and act on it—will help you and honor the person giving you the feedback. That is why I see this process as a "virtuous cycle" composed of five steps or stages:

1. **Welcome it.** Let others know that you are open to receiving feedback, especially constructive criticism to help you do your job better.

2. **Listen and absorb.** Show by your body language, facial expression, and tone of voice that you are really listening to what's being said. Don't interrupt with rebuttals and excuses.

3. **Make a plan to modify your behavior.** After you've received some feedback, think about how you can change your behavior.

4. **Make the changes.** When you make changes in your work habits and behavior, others will see by your actions that you value their comments and observations. However, if you're attempting to make a major change in your behavior, do it gradually. For example, if you talk too much in meetings, you don't want to go silent. If you need to be more responsive, you don't want to become impulsive. If you go too far too fast, it will seem insincere, and you won't be able to sustain it.

5. **Welcome more feedback.** Seeing the changes you've made, others will be encouraged to give you even more feedback, which will help you continue your goal of meaningful self-improvement.

This is a "virtuous cycle" that continues throughout your career, a slow but steady spiral that takes you upward to increase your skills and experience and then outward to expand your contribution. With the knowledge of your strengths and weaknesses, what you've mastered, and where you need to develop, you can seek out what you need. The place you will undoubtedly turn to, time and time again, is the HR department.

SUCCESS SECRETS

➤ Don't underestimate the power of HR.

➤ Distinguish yourself by volunteering for the "dirty work" and unglamorous jobs.

➤ You can progress faster and farther vertically by first moving horizontally.

➤ Be proactive in your performance appraisal; don't wait for your boss to start the process.

➤ When you receive feedback, accept it and act on it.

PART IV:
THE NEW MANAGER

8

THE FIRST-TIME
MANAGER

**When you become a new manager, the skills that got
you there are not what will keep you successful.**

You've been out of college for a few years and, after proving what you
can do on the job, you've been promoted to become a team leader or
manage a department. At this moment in your career, you're under-
going an important shift as you take on your first experience of managing and leading others.

As a new manager, many of the skills that made you successful in
the past (and that may have been the reason you were promoted to
manager) are no longer critical for you. Now, your success as a manager will become dependent on how well your team performs. Their
skills and abilities to do the job will be more important than your
aptitude for the same tasks. In other words, you've moved on to the
next level, and new and different things will be required of you.

At the same time, you've just become the person to whom others
will look for their next raise or promotion. While you may have some
limited experience as a team leader or project leader, perhaps as a
summer job or as part of an assignment, this will be the first time that

you will have direct influence over others' professional lives. Now, not only do you have your own career to manage, you also have other people to worry about.

Becoming a successful, motivating, and highly effective manager takes years of experience. It may even take you a few years to begin feeling comfortable and confident in this new role, particularly if you are managing people who are older than you. To help you make the most of your time as a new manager—to further your progress along this phase of the "understanding curve"—it's important to know what *not* to do. In fact, I believe that being aware of the common "rookie mistakes" that managers make will help you be more effective in your job and increase your contribution to your company, your department, and the team you're leading.

Rookie Mistakes to Avoid

The rookie mistakes described in this chapter are the "default mode" of behavior that most new managers fall back to unless they are made aware of these pitfalls. If these mistakes are not addressed early on, they can seriously undermine a manager's effectiveness and confidence—and potentially derail a promising career.

Mistake No. 1—Reluctance to Delegate

As a new manager, your field of responsibility has broadened tremendously. But with this change comes a shift in your day-to-day activities, including the need to delegate some tasks and responsibilities. This includes work that you've become highly proficient at and for which you've earned some very positive feedback. Admittedly, it's hard to let go of what you're good at. After all, you've just invested all this time and effort into developing an expertise, which is what distinguished you in the first place!

"...(R)eluctance to delegate assignments also has its roots in some very real fears. First is the fear of losing stature: If I assign high-profile projects to my staff members, they'll get the credit. What kind of visibility will I be left with? Will it be clear to my boss and my staff what value I'm adding?" wrote Carol A. Walker, president of Prepared to Lead, a management consulting firm in Weston, Mass.

"Second is the fear of abdicating control: If I allow Frank to do this, how can I be sure that he will do it correctly? In the face of this fear, the rookie manager may delegate tasks but supervise Frank so closely that he will never feel accountable," she added.[61]

Some well-respected authorities and even some people in the business press advise young managers to continue building on their strengths. I take the opposite view: Delegate what you've mastered so that you can broaden your skills and expertise. One of the real issues for rookie managers who suddenly find themselves with wider responsibilities—perhaps even for several teams or departments—is that they focus on where they came from. The reason is simple: that's where their strengths lie. This is a clear case of if you don't delegate, you lose.

Delegating what you've already mastered frees you up to learn something else. Moreover, with your existing expertise, you are in a better position to help others master those skills and attain a higher level of proficiency. This is a concrete example of servant leadership in action: empowering your team members to excel and discover new skills. At the same time, you will expand your competency and efficiency as a manager. It will take you less time to review work that you're the most familiar with than tasks that are new to you.

Delegating and developing your team members, however, can raise a host of your own fears about being overshadowed by someone else. The important thing, however, is not to give in to that fear. This would be detrimental to the individual's development, the team's contribution, the company's talent pool, and your own reputation as a manager.

William G. Bowen, president of The Andrew W. Mellon Foundation and former president of Princeton University, had this advice for young managers: "When young professionals move into a position of some authority and managerial responsibility, it's absolutely key that they not be afraid of good people. There are those who are afraid that they are going to be shown up by someone smarter and more persuasive than they are. The right attitude, however, is that you want to surround yourself with people who can do what you cannot do. If you encourage them, then everyone will thrive," he said.[62]

Mistake No. 2—Prejudging People's Productivity

Delegating does raise another issue that confronts young managers and even some experienced ones: your frustration with the performance of others who are taking over delegated tasks. How fast should they complete these tasks and handle these responsibilities? Should they be as fast as you or slower than you? If slower, by how much? This is a trickier proportion than you may think, because it forces you to put yourself in another person's position.

It's even more difficult to gauge tasks and responsibilities that are unfamiliar to you. (If you delegate what you already know and focus on what you don't, this gives you an advantage.) Otherwise, how can you realistically place expectations on people doing a job you have never done? What kind of expectations can you place on other people?

Begin by observing and asking questions. What are the existing benchmarks around the organization for performance? What pace of work and level of expectations already exist? Once you know what the norm is, you have a baseline for your own expectations. For a young manager, it's always best to start with the status quo, particularly as you get a feel for the breadth and depth of the jobs and responsibilities in your department.

Furthermore, start with the assumption that your direct reports are already competent and are performing at or above expectations. Assume that the people who work for you are good until they prove otherwise. Seek out opportunities to mentor others. This is a perfect way to give back the mentoring you've received and increase your contribution to the organization.

This attitude has a strategic payoff as well. When you expect the best from others and assume that they are producing at a high level, they are more apt to rise to the level of those expectations. Assuming that people are below the grade and need to prove themselves worthy can be both demoralizing and counterproductive. This "expect the best" attitude has been proven not only in my own experience, but in research as well. J. Sterling Livingston, a former Harvard Business School professor and founder of the Sterling Institute, found that the boss's expectations played a key role in the results that were achieved.

"Some managers always treat their subordinates in a way that leads to superior performance. But most managers...unintentionally treat their subordinates in a way that leads to lower performance than they are capable of achieving," Livingston wrote. "The way managers treat their subordinates is subtly influenced by what they expect of them. If managers' expectations are high, productivity is likely to be excellent. If their expectations are low, productivity is likely to be poor."[63]

As a new manager, your team's performance will directly reflect your own attitude. Instead of prejudging others as lacking, a new manager would do well to start with his or her own attitude.

Mistake No. 3—"Saving Souls"

As you evaluate your team, you will almost always find someone who is just not up to par with the others. At this point, as the manager, you need to determine whether this person can be retrained or coached.

Would redefining the job or changing responsibilities in the department make a difference? As the manager, you have to ask the deep question: Is the employee passionate about the work? If so, insist that he or she develop a plan to improve performance. In the end, you'll know whether the person can be helped or if this is a case of someone in the wrong job.

While this can be a very difficult and potentially painful experience, you cannot "save" people by keeping them in a job in which they cannot or will not perform. The person needs to be relieved of that position so that he or she can find a job that's a better fit. Unless you take the necessary steps, however, that won't happen.

Before taking any action, you need to ascertain why and how this person ended up in your department. Often, a story exists that you may not be aware of—and sometimes circumstances that may preclude you from taking any further action. For example, is the person a long-time employee who has been moved around many times, and now upper management has decided that this person will stay on your team until retirement? Or does the person have some connection to someone higher up in the organization, which means you cannot terminate him or her? You won't be aware of any behind-the-scenes issues unless you ask and someone tells you.

Trying Too Hard to "Save Souls"

In my own career, I've had to fight the temptation to "save souls," particularly if I believed that someone was capable of performing up to expectations. I remember one manager, a foreign national, who was transferred from an overseas operation to the U.S. I believed that if I worked with this man long enough, he could adapt his style to the U.S. operating environment. I tried unsuccessfully for years to coach him. Finally, I could see that this was not working. He was far too entrenched in his style and mode of operating to change. Ultimately I had to recommend to the board of directors that this person be let go. As a result, the man took the option of retiring early.

One of the company's directors called me aside and gave me valuable advice. He said, "Bill, you've done a good job up to this point, but you have to be less of a saver of souls. There are times when things just don't work out."

The lesson I learned was that you have to make an honest effort to determine if you can coach someone through a difficult transition or a lackluster performance. But if that individual doesn't improve in a reasonable amount of time, you have to face the facts. It comes down to an issue of balance between moving too quickly and not giving someone the chance he or she deserves and waiting too long, which ultimately wastes the person's time and yours. Dealing with people issues promptly and directly is not only good for them, it's also fair to the rest of the organization. If one person is stuck and not evolving as he or she should, that person is also blocking other people's growth.

Mistake No. 4—When You Can't Fix a Problem

With a little persistence and the right attitude, any problem can be fixed. Right? Wrong. This fact may be hard for an enthusiastic and idealistic manager to swallow. However, in most companies (if not all), long-term, enduring issues persist that you, as a young manager, will face. These problems are often endemic, like a pesky competitor you can't get rid of or a technology in the marketplace that exceeds yours. That's not to say you should shrug off every challenge you encounter. You need to know when to tackle a problem head-on and when it's futile to refuse to accept defeat. Some problems—for the time being, anyway—won't go away.

When you encounter such a situation, discuss it with your boss. Find out the history behind the issue and the problem. You may also learn that your boss has the very same frustrations you have. One of the solutions is to look for little pieces of the problem that you can solve. By "eating around the edges" of the bigger problem, you may find that, in time, you can reduce the size of the overall situation to one that can finally be addressed.

This is reminiscent of the challenge faced by the Japanese auto industry as it began competing in the U.S. market, which had been dominated by General Motors and Ford. The Japanese companies knew the competition problem they faced was too large to tackle head-on. Instead, they found a niche in which they could gain a foothold, producing high-quality, lower-cost small cars, which GM and Ford did not feature. From this initial step, they gained smaller pieces of the market until they were able to mount a larger competitive challenge.

Mistake No. 5—Pet Projects That No One Cares About

As a new manager, you'll set priorities for your team or department. With this responsibility comes the temptation to follow your own agenda of pet projects instead of focusing on the the organization's bigger goals. It may be the area in which you really shine, or something you like doing. But be honest with yourself: Are you on a tangent that's unimportant or is in a different direction than the company's goals? You can rationalize it all you want, but if these pet projects don't serve the greater good and are not aligned with the company's objectives, you are not doing your best as a manager.

Some companies, such as 3M, historically have allowed managers and engineers to spend up to 15 percent of their work time on pet projects. If your company does that, you're in luck. Otherwise, if you need help evaluating these projects, seek your boss's feedback. As a new manager, you'll be pursuing open communication with your boss and welcoming feedback. Let your boss know what priorities you have set, and make sure that you're on target with the bigger objectives.

Mistake No. 6—Moving Too Fast

Another common mistake for new managers is the belief that they have to show they are "the boss." Usually, they think the way to do that is to make major decisions quickly, often without the proper analysis, in hopes of looking aggressive. Or they strive for a sense of urgency by making decisions without consulting others whose approval should be sought. (Decision-making is addressed later in this chapter.)

This may involve giving raises quickly to people on the team who claim to be underpaid. This is the usual scenario: As soon as a new manager takes over, someone (or a few people) says, "I'm so glad you're the boss! Your predecessor never did the job right. Now that you're here, things will be much better." And then the litany of complaints begins: "You know, I haven't gotten the raises I was promised."

If you try to look decisive by granting raises to "correct" an outstanding problem, you run the risk of making decisions too soon, for the wrong reasons, and without the necessary approval. Many of the people who will approach you with a list of complaints and injustices are the whiners who are really underperforming. Chances are the raises they were supposedly promised were mostly in their imagination. Before making a rash decision, take the time to observe your staff and figure out who is a true performer and who is an opportunist.

Moving too quickly in decisions may be rooted in the desire to look like a "dynamic leader." That motivation, in itself, is a problem. If you find yourself wondering, "What are the biggest challenges to becoming a dynamic leader?," you've answered your own question. The problem is in trying too hard.

Don't worry about being "dynamic." Do what's expected of you as a new manager. Make sure you're in sync with your boss's objectives and the company's goals. Make your team's success your first priority.

Making Decisions

Now that you know the rookie mistakes to avoid, it's time to address the attitudes, behaviors, and habits that will make you an effective manager who can lead others and increase your level of contribution. One essential area for new managers is making decisions. This encompasses knowing what you can and cannot decide on your own, seeking input, and implementing a decision with confidence.

The challenge for some managers is that with this newfound authority they believe they have been "knighted" and no longer need anyone's approval before marching off on their own quest. This is a very flawed attitude. The truth is that some decisions will always exist for which you need approval. Even if you become the CEO someday, certain decisions will require the approval of the company's board of directors. It's that simple.

So how do you find out what decisions you can and cannot make without approval? Ask your boss. Then, as you begin evaluating things in your department or area, you will come up with ideas and actions that you want to put into motion. You can bring these to your boss for discussion and approval. You'll get feedback (see Chapter 7, "Developing Your Career"), and in time you may be given more authority to operate independently. As a new manager, however, make sure you know the parameters of your decision-making authority.

When you are privy to the broader decision-making process, know where your input is appropriate and where it is not. Offering an opinion just for the sake of "looking smart" is not a wise move if you are talking about areas in which you have no experience or direct involvement. Know what your role is and when your experience is not broad or deep enough to add value to the whole organization.

As Greg Maddux, the Chicago Cubs pitcher, told me, "I get asked from time to time by management, should we get this player or that player. I can't comment on something like that. It's not my money to spend, and I believe that. I'm just glad that they gave me a job. I'll do the best job I can and do all I can to make the team better.... You have to play by the rules. There will be times when you can use your own imagination and creativity, when it will work best for both sides."[64]

As you make decisions, understand that your attitude says even more than the words you use to communicate it. If your decision appears to have been made effortlessly, others will follow you more readily. If you have trouble with this and you tend to agonize over decisions, make sure you don't show that internal struggle.

Understand, too, that to be a good decision-maker, you must use a combination of logic and instinct. In other words, you may have reached the logical conclusion or the answer that is dictated by the data, but that decision must still "feel" right. While some managers go by their "feeling" about something, this is not the optimal way to make decisions. You must have the right combination of facts and instinct to make a good decision, to have confidence in it, and to communicate it to others believably and with authority.

In your decision-making process, sometimes you will seek additional input. My former boss, Jack Gray, believed strongly in having a dialogue with people about issues and keeping an open mind if someone could convince him with a well-founded argument. A strong manager is one who is perceived as willing to invite and accept input. After all, you are the team leader whose job it is to set the pace, prioritize the tasks, and monitor the progress. You're not expected to be a genius who knows everything. When you seek input from others, however, you must be sincere.

As my mentor, Professor Georges Doriot, frequently said, "Don't ask people for their input if your mind is already made up." You may have strong feelings one way or the other, but if you still have an open mind and can accept input, do so. Of course, if your boss is the one giving you the input, and he or she doesn't agree with your point of view, you should listen carefully to the argument. As you receive and filter the input, trust your ability to make a final decision.

As a new manager, it's good to seek input from many sources, including some more experienced members of your staff. Keep in mind that input is not a "vote." The best managers I know establish decision guidelines for when they need to seek out information to make their own decision, when they invite a group decision, or when they issue a directive.

What happens to inexperienced managers, however, is that the conflicting opinions make it difficult to reach a conclusion. As a result, they may make decisions based on the last person who talked to them. This insidious habit shows a lack of conviction and an inability to take a stand. You may not recognize this tendency in yourself, but everyone else does.

The Boss Who Couldn't Say "No"

The flip side of receiving valuable input in your decision-making process is a frustrating problem I ran into as a manager many years ago. I had a boss who would seemingly agree with everything I was proposing, all through our dialogue and my presentations. He'd never say no, although he never said yes outright either.

His body language and his demeanor gave me the clear message that he was in agreement. With this understanding, I would go forward with what I was pursuing, right up to the point of needing his final approval or signature on a contract. That's when he'd finally get around to saying no. What I learned from that frustrating experience is the value of letting people know, up front, when I disagreed with them.

While seeking additional input before making a decision is a good practice, don't go to the extreme. Believing that you can't make a decision unless you have every fact and consider every possible scenario will render you powerless to make a decision. It's the old "paralysis by analysis" scenario. This is where experience and balance come in, and you may get some coaching on this from more seasoned managers or even your boss. While you don't want to act impulsively, you don't want to agonize to the point of being unable to make a decision.

Don't be afraid to make decisions in increments. Rather than changing everything—reassigning jobs or completely changing the work flow—you can break things down in steps and see what happens. Remember, you can always speed up the pace of change. But if you slow it down, you'll throw your decision-making into question. You may inadvertently raise suspicion among your team members about "what else might be going on" that caused this sudden change in pace. Making decisions incrementally also helps counter a common rookie error of second-guessing the decision once it's made. This may stem from a lack of confidence or a lack of experience, but it can dog a manager throughout his or her career.

Also know when the proper decision is to say no rather than promising everybody that "we'll look into that" or "I'll take that to management for consideration." Probably some bona fide issues in your department need to be presented to your boss for consideration. However, it's not your job to gather everybody's issues, complaints, and problems and dump them on someone else's desk. You are not an "agent"; you can make decisions, and it's your responsibility to discern what needs to be addressed and what really isn't a problem. Then you can decide what you can deal with yourself, within your parameters of responsibility, and what you need your boss's input to address.

Your Management Style

Your decision-making process is part of a broader scope of attitudes and behaviors that, taken together, form your management style. For example, are you the type who is very demanding when it comes to results? Or are you the kind of manager who believes in coaching others to help them do the best job possible?

Your management style, to a great degree, reflects your personality. For example, some people are naturally "hardwired" to be more persuasive, while others are nurturing. The question is, does this natural style fit into the organization and the area in which you're working? This may be less of an issue if you have moved into the role of manager within the company. If you were hired from the outside, however, you need to determine whether your natural management style is one that your company's culture affirms and embraces.

Feedback from a trusted advisor will help you evaluate your management style and identify where your rough edges are. Your basic style of managing, however, is not likely to change. It's up to you to be honest with yourself as to whether this department or company is a good fit for you or if you need to seek another opportunity that will suit you better.

In your career, after you've been promoted from being an individual contributor to a manager, you may find that the position is not a good fit. You may be far more comfortable and effective operating on your own than being responsible for a team or department. Or the corporate culture could change after a merger or acquisition. If that happens, it's okay to admit this isn't a good fit and to look for a new opportunity where you can contribute using your strengths. Some very talented individuals can make a great contribution and enjoy success as individual contributors.

Meeting Your Team

The first days on the job as a new manager are both exciting and nerve-racking, no matter what your rank is in an organization. In this new position, you have high expectations for yourself and your team and a deep commitment to making a contribution. At the same time, you have to face an element of uncertainty: How will you and your direct reports get along?

Luckily, tried-and-true advice for young managers will help ease this transition. The first step is to make sure you meet your team face-to-face and one-on-one as soon as possible. In my career, whenever I took on a new management position, I devoted much of my first days on the job to meeting with everyone. I wanted the opportunity to introduce myself and to get to know them. In this first, critical round of meetings, understand that you gain respect by giving it. The primary message that you should communicate is that you sincerely care about them and their needs. When your team members believe they are your top priority, you will be rewarded with their respect, confidence, and loyalty.

As you interact with your team, let them know that you welcome their feedback. Your company may have a formal or informal way of doing that. Your approach, however, should be to encourage honest and open feedback and to receive it without being defensive. Probably one of the most memorable pieces of feedback I ever received was that I was impatient. Knowing that about myself, and how it made others around me feel about themselves, I was able to correct my behavior. It's not that I instantly became a patient manager. Rather, I monitored how I spoke and acted. Believe me, the only time you get to be impatient is when you're the CEO! As a young manager, it was better for me to understand what was involved with a certain task or project, including how my team performed its duties, than to simply ask for it to be accomplished more quickly.

As you meet your team, you may find that you are managing workers who are older than you. It's not uncommon for a newly graduated MBA with a few years of work experience to be managing people who are 10, 20, or even 30 years older than they are. This can be quite a challenge for everyone involved!

Asking for Advice from and Dealing with Older Workers

When you're a fresh manager in a new assignment, you'll have to learn many things, particularly about "how things work" in the company or a particular department or division. You know that, and so does your team. So how do you deal with older workers, who have more experience in the company and whom you're supposed to manage? The answer is simple: Ask for advice.

Believe me, nothing melts an old-time tough guy's heart faster than the sincere request, "Can you give me some help and advice?" One caveat, however, is that the older workers will know in a nanosecond whether you're being sincere.

Remember that these older, more experienced workers have seen a lot of managers come and go. The first assumption they will probably make is that you, like your predecessors, won't be around for very long. After a few years, you'll move on to something else. Your responsibility as the new manager is to show a level of commitment to them that indicates that you plan on being around for a long time—or at least to act like it. Your attitude will be a welcome change and will give your team members the security that you are committed to them and to making positive changes on their behalf.

Managing Your Boss

As you become a manager, chances are you will have a new boss. Just as you did as a new employee, you will have to initiate communication with your new boss. Now that you're a boss, you'll have a lot more empathy for your boss! You'll understand the pressures that come from having direct reports, who are looking to you for direction, guidance, and their next promotion or raise. You'll appreciate that bosses are people, too.

One of the key components of your relationship with your boss is to make him or her look good through the contribution made by you and your team. Too often, young managers want to make a name for themselves, and they are concerned that their bosses will take credit for what they're doing. My advice is, don't worry about it. True, sometimes bosses take credit for your work; I've seen it happen. Chances are, however, that other people will notice that your boss is suddenly smarter—ever since you joined the team. Ultimately, your boss will probably recognize how valuable you are and how committed you are to leading your team.

What happens, however, when your boss is off-target? Your boss, for whatever reason, seems to have a different agenda and is going in a different direction. What should you do? Robert E. Kelley, Ph.D., a professor at Carnegie Mellon's Graduate School of Industrial Administration and a consultant to major companies, suggested that young managers "keep an eye on the boss." "If you don't," he added, "you put yourself at risk."[65]

As a first step, the manager can try to satisfy the boss's demands while making sure that his team's work is still focused on the company's main objectives. If the problem becomes more severe, it's time to seek out confidential advice from a trusted mentor or an advisor in HR or elsewhere at the company. It could be that your boss has a personal agenda that is different from the company's agenda. Perhaps the boss still wants to pursue a new technology, an operating plant, or a product that the company has already turned down. The boss may believe that, in time, management will come around to his or her way of thinking.

With your advisor's help, you will be able to come up with the best course of action for you, your department, and your boss. Don't try to go it alone in these situations. You need the perspective of someone with more experience and a broader perspective—someone you know and trust.

Personal Selling and Negotiating

By the time you become a manager, you should have some experience with both personal selling and negotiating. These two skills will serve you well throughout your career. Your personal selling involves making a pitch, whether on behalf of yourself or your team. You could be selling an idea to your boss, to your boss's boss, or one day to the executive office or the board of directors. It may be a new technology, an improved compensation system, an innovative marketing idea, or another proposal. Whatever you're pitching, you must have some skills in personal selling to communicate the benefit of your idea and what it entails.

The key skills in personal selling are listening to a particular problem that a customer has, understanding the situation, and then creating a solution that will add value. This is in contrast to trying to push your product or services on someone by convincing him that he needs it.

A closely related area is negotiation, particularly as you try to meet the needs of your team or department and others within the company. You may be negotiating with an outside vendor, an advertising agency, or with your boss on a project timeline or to promote someone. Or you could be dealing with other managers who want to hire a member of your team. (Having other people in the company hire away your staff is a credit to you if you are seen as a manager who develops his or her team members.)

Selling and negotiating are inextricably linked, revolving around the concept of understanding a problem from the other person's perspective. You'll find that the best salespeople are good listeners and skilled problem solvers. They negotiate by using "alternative currencies," offering one thing for another.

Using "Alternative Currencies"

Nathan, a vice president of marketing, used a combination of education and personal comfort in exchange for buyers' valuable time and attention. Every year buyers for major retail chains from across the country would come to the Housewares Show in Chicago, at which Nathan's company was an exhibitor. Instead of only exhibiting at a booth at the show, Nathan came up with a novel idea to get the buyers' attention and earn their loyalty by offering something that was valuable to them: education.

Nathan put together a mini-seminar on topics such as store layout, different kinds of store fixtures, facing and displaying products, and the importance of return on investment over the cost of acquiring products. Before the Housewares Show, the buyers were all contacted, invited to the seminar, and asked about their travel arrangements. Then, when they arrived at O'Hare International Airport in Chicago, greeters hired by the company met the people at the gate and escorted them to a suite at the airport hotel to attend the seminar. Other handlers from the company fetched their luggage and put it into waiting limousines. At the end of the program, which included only a small presentation about the company's products (and some refreshments), the buyers were escorted to the limousines and taken to their hotels.

The first year Nathan tried this approach, a few buyers took him up on the offer. The second year, many more buyers participated. By the third year, buyers were calling Nathan well in advance to inquire about that year's seminar. The goodwill he established by offering the seminars and the hassle-free comfort of getting to the hotel paid off in increased loyalty and more business from these buyers.

As you negotiate with customers, both inside and outside your company, consider the kind of "alternative currencies" you can use. Time, resources, talent, a service, or convenience may be highly valued by your customer and readily at your disposal.

As you approach personal selling and negotiating, think a level or two higher than just the immediate situation. Think about why you want to sell a particular idea, concept, project, or product. How does this fit into the larger scale for the customer, whether it's someone inside the company who must "buy into" your idea or an external customer who is considering a product or service you're offering? The more you can think from the customer's perspective, the better salesperson you will be by truly solving problems. The key is to offer something of value to the other party that you can easily deliver.

Creating a Positive Environment

As a young manager, you have a critically important perspective: You remember what it was like, not so long ago, to be an entry-level employee or a member of the team without any real authority. With that knowledge, you can create a motivating environment for your direct reports and team members.

The root of your success will be your ability to shift your perspective as you undergo a major, and most likely permanent, transition from an individual performer to a manager. Instead of focusing solely on what you can do, your contribution as a manager is leveraged and magnified through the efforts of others. This will require you to delegate tasks at which you are proficient, to help others develop their expertise in areas you have mastered, and to challenge yourself to take on new duties and assignments.

To ease your transition in becoming a manager, be aware of the rookie mistakes to avoid, as well as the habits and behaviors that will help you become more effective. Above all, don't forget what it was like to be on the team and to have a boss to manage. Now that you're in that role, others are trying to manage their relationships with you! Your awareness and willingness to create a positive team environment can establish a successful relationship for all involved.

SUCCESS SECRETS

➤ Delegate what you know and have mastered in order to develop yourself—and your team.

➤ Don't be afraid to set high expectations; people can usually meet them.

➤ Make your boss look good.

➤ When making decisions, know when you need approval and when you don't.

➤ Every management style is valuable; the trick is to match it to the situation.

➤ Don't be afraid to ask for advice.

➤ You must be an effective salesperson, inside and outside the company.

9

BUILDING YOUR TEAM

"Star performers are never expensive, but mediocre performers are unaffordable."

—Georges Doriot

You probably want your team to be composed of all high-performing superstars who excel at their tasks and exceed expectations. However, that is not how it works in the real world. You are more likely to find that most of the people on your team are not stars, and some of them never will be. Rather, teams are more often heterogeneous mixes of people, some of whom are better than others. Some teams and individuals can be coached to a higher level of performance; others never will make the grade.

As a young manager, taking a good hard look at the team you inherited can be disillusioning. You may see a mix that is not that appealing. The good news, however, is that virtually every manager is confronted with the same reality. Therefore, if you strive to build a team that can make even a slightly better contribution to the company, this will have a significant impact on the organization. Know too that you don't need to get every member of your team up to the next level. Probably only six to ten people report directly to you. If only one or two improve, the positive impact will be greatly leveraged by the whole team.

Your job as a manager is to continually build your team, making improvements in performance whenever and wherever you can. Some members who are not performing up to standard will be replaced. They will either change jobs themselves, or they will be terminated. You may have some direct reports, including some of your best performers, who are recruited away from your team to other departments or even to other companies. Thus, your job of culling, improving, and motivating your team is an ongoing one.

Team building has two essential elements: one is coaching and developing; the other is hiring. As important as these activities are, you won't be 100 percent successful with either of them. When it comes to being coached, only a small percentage of people will really "get it" and make determined efforts to change their habits, modify their behavior, and stretch themselves to reach new levels of effectiveness. With your hiring, you won't be nearly as good at interviewing and selecting people as you think you are or want to be.

As disappointing as this may be, the good news is a little improvement goes a long way. If you can coach even a few individuals to better performance, this can make a significant difference to your team and to the company. Similarly, even a small improvement in your ability to interview and select people will make a tremendous impact. Let's take a look at some of the specific areas of team building, starting with one area in which most managers are lacking: adding the right players to the team.

Selecting People for Your Team

When you are faced with the need to hire someone, the first consideration is where to find the best candidates. One of the most effective techniques is to keep a list of the people you've met and their particular interests or talents (see Chapter 3, "Your Network: It's All About 'Giving,' Not Just 'Getting'"). Look for people who are diverse, but will complement your existing team. Recognize that individual members have unique roles to play based on their personality types and experience. For your high-performance team, you may need to bring in a "producer" to energize the group, a "creative" to spark new ideas, a "controller" to pay more attention to detail, and so forth. Ethnic and gender diversity is not only a good business practice, it can also strengthen your team.

By keeping in contact with people—including former associates, classmates, and others—you will know about their successes, strengths, accomplishments, and career progression. Furthermore, they will know about top people in their fields. Your list will include people inside your company and outside. As you look for candidates, consider first the people within the company, since the goal of most organizations is to develop their internal resources. Moreover, their track record of skills, expertise, and contribution are already known, as are their faults.

The 60 Percent Rule

As you evaluate potential candidates to fill an opening on your team, one person comes to mind: Sarah is already inside the company and has a proven track record of accomplishments. She's an eager learner, is well liked by others, and her manager speaks highly of her. There's only one problem: Sarah doesn't have all the skills and experience needed to join your team. She is, however, more than halfway qualified.

This is where the "60 Percent Rule" comes into play. If you can determine that someone who is already inside the company is at least 60 percent ready to take the job, is well liked and respected, and is supported by people around her who would feel she's a good fit for the job, hire her.

Once Sarah is in the job, she will need to fill out the other 40 percent of knowledge, skills, and experience. The people around her, however, will coach her and step in if she gets into a bind. That is a virtual guarantee of Sarah's success on the job. On the other hand, if you bring in some hotshot from outside the company who appears to be 110 percent ready for the job, people on the team may resent this outsider and do nothing to help him.

In order for the internal candidate to be a good fit, however, the 60 Percent Rule—and all its qualifying conditions—must be met.

Taking a chance on a promising internal candidate who may not be fully ready for the job can have many benefits all the way around. You will get credit for helping promote and develop internal talent, your new hire will be highly motivated to perform, and your boss will be happy with the positive outcome.

When considering an internal candidate who is not quite ready for the job, make sure you weigh carefully the organizational support that this person is likely to receive. In other words, how will people feel about this person being promoted or hired by another department? Will she be coached and supported by her colleagues? Or will he be left on his own, to make mistakes without anyone's stepping in to help? While a lack of expertise or skill can be made up with coaching from colleagues, this important development will not occur if someone, for whatever reason, lacks the support of the organization.

Consider the case of "Martin," who was hired as a customer service representative at a large financial services company. From the start, he let it be known that he was moving up in the company. He went out of his way to ingratiate himself with every team leader, supervisor, and boss. But Martin never cared about his team and all but ignored his colleagues. Martin finally got his wish and was promoted to become the leader of another team. While he was very bright and had mastered the job he came from, he was still on a learning curve. Technically, he was 60 percent ready but needed the support of his new team to succeed. His reputation preceded him, and no one on that team went out of his or her way to help him. After a year, Martin left the company.

Bringing "Your" Team Onboard

As a manager looking to build your team, you will face the big temptation to bring in "your" people from inside and outside the company. Unless you're in a turnaround situation, in which new talent must be brought in immediately, some very real drawbacks exist to bringing in your own team. (In addition to a turnaround, another possible exception is in financial services, where it's not uncommon for an entire team or trading desk to move in tandem.)

For one thing, you don't want to decimate the ranks of the department you came from by moving over the heart of the team. Maybe you want to recruit one person, or possibly two. You must make sure, however, that the person you're bringing in is vitally important to this new operation and not just a "buddy" or part of your comfort zone. If someone is truly a specialist who can add value to an operation, consider recruiting that person—obviously after checking with the current boss first. Otherwise, look at your existing pool of talent to see who can be developed with training and coaching.

Don't give the impression that you can only work with "your" people. That can be demoralizing and counterproductive for the existing people in the department. They'll be concerned that their jobs are on the line—even if they're not—and their performances will likely suffer out of fear that they won't be around for much longer.

The worst example is to load your team with friends and former classmates. The simple advice is don't do it. You and your friend may be convinced that you can handle this dual relationship and that your friendship won't interfere with your professional life and vice versa. The problem arises, however, when you have to discipline that person or give him or her some particularly tough feedback. If you have a personal connection, it becomes too difficult.

If you think you're helping your friends by hiring them, you're actually hurting them. You could be tempted to let poor performance slide and not adequately challenge them to excel. Overall, the best thing to do for your friends is to encourage them to seek their fame and fortune working for someone else.

Interviewing Skills

Once the candidates for the job have been identified, including some people from outside the company, it's time for the job that most managers don't adequately prepare for and handle poorly—interviewing. Unfortunately, too many managers don't realize that they do a poor job of interviewing people. They may believe that they are so good at managing and motivating people that this automatically makes them good at interviewing and selecting the right candidates. These skill sets, however, are completely different. Even if someone is a gifted manager, a patient coach, and a real champion for his team, he may not possess the right skills for being a good interviewer. Or she may be so busy with the day-to-day running of her team that she doesn't take the time to brush up on her interviewing skills by taking a course or role-playing with someone in human resources.

That's where you as a young manager can take positive steps to consciously improve your interviewing skills. This is one area that you *don't* want to delegate. When it comes to interviewing, you already have an advantage. You remember what it was like to go through interviews (see Chapter 4, "Finding Your Ideal Position") and to deal with managers who weren't very good at the process. This should give you the motivation to become more skilled at interviewing.

If you're concerned about having enough time to develop this skill, ask yourself what's getting in the way. If you are handling too many of your team's day-to-day duties, it's time to delegate. See who can take some of these responsibilities. The person will benefit from the opportunity to develop expertise in a new area, and you will free yourself to acquire better skills as a manager. Your company will benefit in both instances.

Even if you continually upgrade your interviewing skills, don't expect that you'll have a 100% success rate with your hiring, or even 80% or 70%. The members of a university advisory council composed of experienced businesspeople were asked to estimate their personal success rate in hiring. Most of them said about 50%. Although this is anecdotal, it's important to note that these senior people did not see themselves as having a stellar track record hiring. (If 50% seems low, remember the old saying about baseball: You need to have a hit only four times out of ten to make it to the Hall of Fame!) With your hiring, if you're batting .400—being "right" 40% of the time—you don't have to aim for the impossible goal of perfection. If you can improve to a 50% success rate (batting .500), that's a 10 percentage point difference—or a 25% improvement.

The better you become with interviewing and the selection process, the easier your life will be as a manager. You will end up with a mix of people, to be sure. But this creates a greater likelihood of having people who are willing to be coached and of having the potential to make a real contribution. You may even end up with a few superstars.

To add value to what's already been written on interviewing, I want to focus on a few targeted ways to improve your skills and comfort in conducting interviews. At the top of that list is behavioral interviewing, which helps you determine what a person has actually accomplished and the specific contributions he or she made in previous jobs. Someone's résumé may list some impressive-sounding jobs with well-known and respected companies. But was he or she really a valuable employee? Or did he or she coast along on the team's momentum? You can explore these issues by asking open-ended questions such as "What was your role in the project?" and "What problems did you encounter, and how did you address them?" Make sure that you're doing far more listening than talking in the interview, which is the opposite of what you experienced when you were the one interviewed for a job. In fact, you should talk only about 10 to 20% of the time, which you can accomplish if you ask good, open-ended questions.

Another way to make interviews more effective is to extend the session to observe the person in a more relaxed situation. This helps you focus on the person's behavior, not on his or her skill at answering questions. This may be as simple as walking the person to the elevator, to the front door, or even to his or her car. See how he or she carries on a more relaxed conversation. Does he or she acknowledge the receptionist with whom he or she first spoke? Consider inviting the person to lunch or even to have a cup of coffee outside the office. The longer you can spend with a candidate, the more likely it is that the pretenses will come down and you will gain insight into who this person really is and how he or she will fit with your team.

Ted was being recruited to become a general manager at the company, a position in which he could make a tremendous contribution. Making sure he was the right person for the job, therefore, was paramount. After two previous interviews, Ted was being flown in for another meeting with management. That gave me an idea. My wife and I invited Ted and his wife to come in early and spend an entire day with us. It just so happened that the professional baseball team in the city in which we were living at the time was in the playoffs, and I had tickets for the game. Ted and his wife were eager to go.

Unfortunately, it was unseasonably hot that day. As we sat and watched the game, we were drenched with sweat, and our clothes were literally sticking to us. We were sitting in the hot sun, watching an exciting game under the most uncomfortable circumstances. Yet nobody wanted to go before the game was over. When we finally did leave the ballpark, we brought Ted and his wife back to our house before dinner to shower and change clothes (they had to borrow some of ours).

This was not the day we had planned, but Ted and his wife were such good sports. We truly enjoyed their company, and I had a high level of confidence in hiring him. He turned out to be one of the best hires I ever made. The moral of this story is, while you shouldn't go out of your way to artificially create a stressful situation, you can learn a lot about a person when faced with a challenge—even if it's only a hot day at the ball game.

As a final step in the interviewing and screening process, reference checking is effective only if you speak to someone who will candidly discuss the person and his or her performance. The references candidates provide are the names of people who will say nice things about them. More valuable and unbiased feedback needs to be sought out. However, given our litigious society and company policies, this may be difficult to obtain. One way to get around these obstacles is to call someone who is not listed as a reference (perhaps the candidate's former manager) when you know he or she won't be in the office. Leave a voicemail to the effect of "We have been interviewing So-and-So. We believe this person is an outstanding candidate for the job and has the kind of skills and expertise we're looking for. If you think we're making the right decision, please call me back." If you hear from the person, you'll get the confirmation you've been seeking. If you don't hear from the person (particularly if you've left similar messages with two or three people about an individual), you should ask yourself if you're making a mistake.

When the interview process is over, you must make a decision based on the input and feedback you've received. In addition to individual accomplishment, also consider a person's creativity and curiosity, which can lead to innovative solutions and unique approaches.

However, as Professor Georges Doriot used to say, "Always choose an 'A' manager with a 'B' idea over a 'B' manager with an 'A' idea. An 'A' manager can improve a 'B' idea, while almost always a 'B' manager will not deliver on an 'A' idea."

After you've made your decision, keep a record of whom you've hired and what your expectations are. This lays the groundwork for "feedback analysis," which, according to management guru Peter Drucker, will help you identify your successful and not-so-successful hires[66] (see the "Forecasting" section in the Appendix, "Your Toolbox for Success"). Over time, you'll see how often your expectations have been realized and how often the actual results fell short of what you had hoped. Patterns may develop that will be helpful in the future. For example, do you value technical competence over interpersonal skills? Are you too easily impressed with how well a person communicates and overlook what he or she has actually accomplished? When you know your weak spots as an interviewer, you can avoid making the same mistakes.

Delivering Feedback

To build and maintain your team, you have at your disposal some very important and highly effective tools. This includes your observations of how the team is performing and the feedback you can give to individual employees. You remember when you were starting your career how important feedback was to your development. Hopefully, you are still seeking feedback from your peers, your boss, and even your direct reports about your own performance.

As uncomfortable as it was for you to solicit and receive feedback, now you will experience just how difficult it can be to deliver it. "Giving feedback is difficult; it's hard to do well. Giving feedback constructively and effectively may well be one of the most difficult skills to master," observed Frank LaFasto, senior vice president of organization effectiveness at Cardinal Health.[67]

One contemporary technique that is gaining popularity is asking your team members to evaluate their own performance first. That way, you will have feedback from them on how they believe they are performing, where they see their strengths, and what they identify as their development needs. Many times, your direct reports will recognize that they are having a problem with a particular skill or area of responsibility. This opens the door to a discussion that you may have been uncomfortable initiating.

As a manager, at times you will have to give negative feedback to a member of your staff. This can be intimidating, especially the first few times. This should always be done in private and confidentially. The best approach is to be specific about the incident and to address it as quickly as possible. For example, suppose a longtime worker makes a negative comment in a staff meeting and then walks out before the meeting is over. Take time to speak with that employee as soon as possible. Break the ice with a comment such as "At the meeting I saw some good things and some bad things. Do you want my feedback?"

Begin with some positive or neutral feedback. Some experts suggest that you have at least two positives to note before you get into the negatives. For example, "Let's start with the good news first. I thought the meeting was very productive in the beginning, and I appreciated your comments. You asked a very insightful question that moved the discussion along." Then, without getting defensive or showing anger, get to the heart of the issue: "Later on, however, I heard you say, 'We're spending too much time on this unimportant issue' before you walked out of the meeting. Can you tell me what was going on so that we can address it?"

Handling issues in this manner will benefit everybody. First, the employee will feel heard, and you may prevent future outbursts. Second, you will feel empowered to manage difficult situations in a positive manner that benefits your team. To be most effective, this type of feedback should be given immediately, not when it's time for the next review in six months or a year. Feedback loses its potency and relevance the longer you wait.

After you've given your feedback, offer the person support for changing his or her habits. Remember to reinforce the good things and not just catch the bad behaviors. Your desired ratio as a manager would be to give feedback on positive behaviors and actions two or three times more frequently than you point out negative ones that the employee is trying to change. To further the person's development you may also coach him in a particular area or encourage him to take a course to develop a skill. These are the demonstrable ways in which you can show that you are truly committed to your team.

As you deliver feedback to your team, such as part of periodic performance reviews, keep the perspective that what you're giving them is factual, based on observable actions over time. This feedback is intended to help them grow and develop (see Chapter 7, "Developing Your Career").

In addition, as manager, it's important to break the connection between feedback and raises. At some companies the link is so strong, managers use the dreaded phrase "I have to give you this feedback so you can get your raise." Every time these words are uttered, even the most thorough and high-quality feedback is overshadowed by their focus on finding out about the raise. While some managers want to associate performance appraisals with raises to save time, it's far better to address these issues separately.

The real world for a manager is filled with challenges that you may not be prepared for, even if you're coming from the best graduate school program. These issues include difficult personnel issues, such as disciplining an older employee, reining in a high performer who won't follow the rules, dealing with a troublemaker, or breaking the news to an employee who expects to be promoted that he won't get the job.

Carefully prepare and rehearse with a trusted advisor or someone from HR. Although these practice sessions won't be the same as confronting the individual, the more you prepare, the better your discussion. Keep your comments brief and factual, and deliver them without strong emotion. Make sure that the person understands the message and what he needs to do. Assure him that you'll support him as he commits to a plan of action to modify his behavior and make positive changes. If the person isn't open and accepting of this feedback, be sure to have a backup plan, which may include punitive steps.

Positive Firing

It's inevitable for every manager that, sooner or later, you will realize that someone on your team needs to be let go. Once you have determined that retaining and reassignment are out of the question, that you have given the person ample chance to improve to no avail, and that all the necessary documentation is in place, it's time to take action. Before you do anything, however, you must examine your own attitude. If you believe that getting fired is the worst thing that could ever happen to a person, the experience will be painful for you and the employee. If you believe, however, that this is ultimately a positive step that will help this person find the right job, it will be far easier for both of you.

Your mind-set is critical to successfully carrying out one of the most difficult conversations you'll ever have. Here, rehearsal is even more important—not just what you will say, but how you will deliver the message. Deliberately plan when and where you will meet with the person, preferably at a neutral site. Have HR and other resources available for follow-on meetings immediately after. Anticipate the person's reaction, which could range from disbelief to anger.

In this short conversation, it's important to stress that this is a decision, not a discussion. Avoid comments such as "I know how you feel," which invites discussion and wanders into inappropriate territory. The person needs to understand that ample evidence demonstrates that he or she is not working out in the job. Do not get into a discussion about changing the decision or giving the person another chance. The overall tone should be that this is an opportunity for the person to move on to a job that is a better fit.

The Right Mind-set for the Most Difficult Conversation

"Ed," a vice president of sales, had come to the realization that "Sam," a regional sales manager, needed to be terminated. Despite a lot of coaching from Ed, Sam still wasn't performing up to expectations and needed to leave the company.

I did some initial work with Ed on how to proceed with Sam's termination, and Ed rehearsed his remarks in role-playing sessions with human resources.

The day of Sam's termination, Ed came into my office. "I can't do it," he told me. "I can't fire the guy. I'm not emotionally prepared. I'm afraid of what might happen to him. I think you should fire him."

"I can't do that," I told him. "He works for you."

We decided to do it together. It was a difficult conversation, but it went fairly well, and we sent Sam to human resources to find out about his termination package. "I couldn't do this without you," Ed told me. "But now that I've gone through it, I could do the next one."

The point of the story is, no matter how much rehearsal you have or how serious you are about terminating someone, it's extremely difficult if you are not in the right frame of mind.

Another challenge in firing is when the person you're letting go refuses to believe that it's really happening. Facing this situation, you may find your resolve and confidence challenged as the person openly defies your authority. "Gordon" was very intelligent and capable of high potential, but his intellectual arrogance got in the way. Gordon believed he was superior to everyone else, didn't have to take direction, and considered himself very well connected to the upper echelon of management. His performance, however, was under par because he was following his own agenda rather than the department's priorities.

After going through all the right steps, including discussing the decision with upper management, his supervisor called Gordon into a meeting and told him that he was not performing up to the standards of the department and the company. He would be better off pursuing an opportunity elsewhere. Gordon became indignant and then belligerent. He refused to believe that he was being fired. It couldn't happen to him! His performance was great! He knew people in high places.

Gordon was told his termination had been approved by upper management and that he was, indeed, being fired. It was a challenging situation, to say the least, but one that carried an important lesson. Rather than getting defensive and arguing with Gordon, the immediate supervisor held his ground and his conviction that firing Gordon was good for the department and good for him. Gordon was unhappy in his job and would be far better off someplace else.

Creating the Motivated Team

In addition to managing a staff day-to-day, continually developing and culling internal talent, you may also have the opportunity one day to pull together a handpicked team for a specific project. While you will look for individuals with talents, skills, and expertise for the job, your bigger challenge will be to create a motivated and unified team. One way to do this is to recognize the importance of their individual and collective contribution. This will empower your team, helping them stretch their limits and accomplish things they may not have thought possible.

Receiving recognition for their efforts and the satisfaction of a job well done will mean far more than any financial reward they may receive. Ample empirical evidence shows that psychological rewards are the best motivators. Compensation ranks behind such factors as making a contribution, doing meaningful work, and having an opportunity to grow.

As a manager, you want to demonstrate that you genuinely care about the individuals on your team and recognize the unique value each person brings. Furthermore, you want to tailor assignments that play to their strengths and allow them to maximize the contribution they can make.

While you want to be seen as a champion for your team, keep in mind that you will need to maintain a very professional relationship with them. You can go out with your entire staff for a beer after work on occasion. However, you should avoid socializing with only a few people or developing a close friendship with one person on the team. To be a manager with objectivity who can command respect, keep a respectful distance.

Still, you should make every effort to get to know your team. One way to do this is to visit people in their offices, at their desks, and in their cubicles. Professor Doriot called this "visiting people in their cages." When you visit people on their turf, they are apt to be more at ease than if they are called into your office. Plus, it gives you a chance to observe what's on their desks—their photos and mementos—which offers a glimpse into their personal lives and pastimes. "Visiting people in their cages" also brings a strategic benefit. When the discussion is over, you can exit gracefully. If someone comes to your office, it can be more difficult to end the meeting without appearing rude or abrupt.

Organization as a Tool

As you develop your team, one of the areas you will look at is how your staff goes about doing their jobs. What tasks and responsibilities does each person have? Are some people on the team better suited to specific tasks and not others? Should the tasks and responsibilities be grouped in a different way? Making organizational changes to redefine jobs and redistribute tasks is a tool to help motivate your team and to give your staff opportunities to learn new skills and develop expertise.

Organizational changes, however, require the right balance. If you make changes too frequently, your team will not have a chance to settle into their jobs. If you don't make enough changes, the structure becomes rigid, and people fall into a rut. The goal is to have an organization that can adapt to changes in the work environment and perform jobs that are continually morphing to accommodate new tasks, demands, opportunities, and challenges.

As you look at your team, look beyond their current duties and tasks. Consider what each person longs to do because of a particular skill, aptitude, or area of interest. It may be something that's aligned with an outside interest or hobby. The only way to discover someone's dreams is to get to know that person and his or her interests and passions. Knowing that, you can really get creative about utilizing the person's talents and matching him or her to the company's needs.

An operating manager at a plant in California had already distinguished himself as a wonderful supervisor and team leader, but what made him particularly interesting was his talent for and interest in mechanical things, which stemmed from his hobby of collecting and restoring antique trucks. Because of his outside interest, he was always suggesting ways that equipment could be rebuilt and used for a second purpose. Management thought about moving him to the maintenance/engineering department, but he was so valued in the operations chain of command that they didn't want to transfer him.

Instead, management added to his regular job the additional responsibilities of equipment design and working with the engineering staff. That allowed the company to tap the creativity that came from his hobby while enabling him to continue in a job where he was valued.

As effective as reorganizing job assignments can be, it is not a cure-all for personnel problems. At times, no matter how much reorganization you do, it still doesn't work. The reason is probably a "people problem" that can't be solved by changing jobs around. Only after the personnel issue is addressed can the reorganization be effective. In the end, if you have a team of people who understand their roles, like what they are doing, and respect each other, the organizational structure becomes secondary—almost to the point of being meaningless.

As a new manager, you will have many opportunities, with your boss's support, to fit your organization to the strategy of your department or enterprise. For example, if the priority is to deliver faster than your competitor, you will probably train and organize your people so that any one person can do the whole job. If you are trying to minimize costs, you would likely train people to have very deep skills in just one function. While the goal will shape the structure, it still has to work with the people, individual talents, and personalities involved.

Rewarding Superstars

As you build and maintain your team, how do you recognize and reward the real star performers who are making the biggest contribution and having the greatest impact? Never hesitate to reward a superstar on your team. After all, you want to make sure that the person is paid fairly, even if it is slightly off the payroll scale. If this person is truly exceptional, no one else in the organization will take offense if that person is paid more based on performance. (Remember, salary is never kept secret for long in any organization.) People do get upset, however, if someone is paid more than his or her performance dictates.

While you must ensure an appropriate "return on investment" for salary and bonuses, don't be too frugal with the rewards. As Professor Doriot observed, "Star performers are never expensive, while mediocre performers are unaffordable."

His comment underscores why anything you can do to make even modest improvements in the performance of mediocre team members will have a significant impact. A small improvement is leveraged across the team, which will lead to better productivity and lower labor costs. This is all the more reason for a young manager to focus his or her energies on mediocre performers, provided they have the capability and interest in improving.

Keep in mind that compensation can also be used as a motivating factor in the inverse—when a financial reward is withheld temporarily. This is a highly effective but largely underutilized strategy that never fails to get someone's attention, provided that the person understands why the action is being taken and what he or she can do to correct it.

The Carrot and the Stick

Brad was one of the greatest talents anyone at the company had ever seen. A marketing vice president, he was enormously creative and had great potential. Unfortunately, Brad was also very lazy and didn't like to extend himself. He was so good, however, that he could perform fairly well while working at a fraction of his speed and potential. The frustration for his manager, however, was imagining what Brad could do if he really set his mind to it.

No amount of coaching seemed to make a difference to Brad. He had gotten by most of his life operating this way, and as far as he was concerned, he was doing his job. His manager didn't want to give up on Brad, knowing what amazing things he could do if he worked to his full potential. The manager used a carrot-and-stick approach to get Brad's attention and ultimately spark him into action.

After reviewing Brad's performance, his manager explained that he would receive no salary increase. His pay wouldn't be cut, but neither would it be raised. Brad was angry and upset at first (and so was his wife, who for months afterward gave the manager the cold-shoulder at company social gatherings). In the past, Brad had been paid well because he was evaluated on the basis of his potential, not his performance. The zero pay increase got his attention. The manager carefully explained that if Brad wanted to increase his compensation, he had to change his work habits.

Only then did Brad's performance change, to the point that he became a real star. As such, he was well rewarded. While the lesson was painful in the short term, it served Brad well over the years as he continued to operate at a high level.

Your team may not be the ideal mix of high performers, innovative thinkers, and creative geniuses that you would like. Most likely they will range from the mediocre to those who have potential and, occasionally, the exceptional. Over time, your team will change. Some people will leave, on their own or because they are not a good fit. New members will join the team, some of whom will be good hires and some who will be disappointing. And a few may develop and grow, becoming star performers over time.

Instead of being discouraged by the ever-changing mix of people and talents, managers should appreciate the benefit of even one or two team members improving. In a realistic corporate environment, a little improvement goes a long way. Managers who strive to develop their teams while honing their own skills will distinguish themselves for making a measurable and meaningful difference.

SUCCESS SECRETS

➤ Find and develop the talent on the team
you inherit.

➤ Beware the superstar from the outside.

➤ Be very selective when recruiting "your" people,
and never hire friends.

➤ Distinguish yourself by being a skilled interviewer.

➤ Adopt a positive mind-set for delivering feedback.

➤ Diversity is not only good business, but makes for
an effective team.

PART V:
SUCCESS HABITS FOR
A LIFETIME

10

THE SUCCESSFUL LIFE

"We are what we repeatedly do; excellence then is not
an act but a habit."

—Aristotle

You are valued for your contribution and were promoted on the basis
of your accomplishments. You've gone from team member to team
leader. Your sights are set on the next level or the one after that, and
maybe the executive suite someday. In other words, you feel as if
you've made it.

Does that mean you can stop learning, growing, and developing?
Hardly. Lessons to be learned can be found at every stage, from Day
One to retirement and beyond. Many of those lessons have very little
to do with your career per se but have a major impact on your success. Those lessons have to do with how well you achieve balance—
between your personal life and your professional life, between what
you do and who you are. The more balance you have, the better you
can reevaluate circumstances, seize opportunities that arise, and
recover from the setbacks you didn't foresee.

Throughout your career, you will find that certain skills, habits,
attitudes, and behaviors have been helpful to you in the past. You will

identify areas that you need to develop and practice more. Some will be on the edge of your radar screen but not fully in focus yet.

You may find someday (or perhaps you've already experienced it) that you are not 100 percent happy in your current career or job choice. Perhaps you were attracted by a job's financial rewards without giving adequate thought to what the work demands would be. Or maybe you're working in an area that, honestly, doesn't interest you or spark your enthusiasm.

"I encounter so many recent graduates who are quite unhappy in their first or second jobs because they're doing what somebody else wants them to do. Maybe it was for reasons of job status. They have an appointment with a large law firm or consulting group, and the money is good, but the work is frustrating and dissatisfying," commented William G. Bowen, president of The Andrew W. Mellon Foundation and former president of Princeton University. "The question then becomes, how do you get restarted because what you are doing doesn't give you enough satisfaction. If you don't have that satisfaction, whether it's from your paying job or volunteer work, then every day is going to be a long day—and it's not going to be a good day."[68]

The good news is that any day can be "Day One" when you recommit to your goals and vision. Throughout your career you will have many "Day Ones," some externally driven by new jobs, promotions, and career changes, and some internally sparked because of a recommitment to your personal goals. You may even have a "Day One" because of changes in your personal life and the corresponding change in your professional life as well.

Life, after all, is not linear. It is a series of surprises, disappointments, opportunities, deadends, U-turns, and unplanned excursions down paths that bring tremendous satisfaction. So how can you plan for a life like that? The answer is, you can't. It's fine to have objectives and goals that lead you forward, as long as you understand that circumstances will change, sometimes for the better and sometimes for the worse. Keeping an open mind as well as a healthy, balanced life will help you cope with the unexpected and take advantage of the fortuitous.

"While you should be thinking ahead—where step A leads you to step B and so forth—it's awfully important not to overplan," Bill Bowen added. "You can't think that you can control things that you can't control. As a wise friend of mine says, 'Life is what happens when you are planning something else.' It's important to be open to new things, perhaps changes in perceptions or new opportunities, and not to stay with some plan that you developed in the absence of such information. You should have a plan, but it should always be subject to revision."[69]

"Investing" in a Dream

Herman Cain's background in mathematics and computers, including an advanced degree from Purdue University (see Chapter 6, "Is Graduate School Right for You?"), had set him on an upward career path. He eventually became vice president of technology for The Pillsbury Company—an executive post he achieved at the early age of 34.

"I was managing 200 people and a $100 million budget. Then I realized after completing some major assignments that the joy just wasn't there. I wasn't happy," Herman recalled. "I had reached the point where I was making good money. I had security, stock options, and the like, but I was not happy. After much assessment and soul-searching, I discovered that I wanted to run a business. I wanted to be the head of a business."

Herman's management experience did afford him an opportunity to switch gears, out of technology and into the consumer side. But first, he would have to take a dramatic step down in both compensation and prestige to join the lower ranks of the Burger King organization, which at the time was owned by Pillsbury, and learn the ropes of a new business. Eventually, he worked his way up again, becoming a vice president and general manager for Burger

King. He was put in charge of 400 restaurants in the Philadelphia area that were, at the time, among the worst-performing units in the chain. Three-and-a-half years later, they were among the best.

"It was a risk. But I couldn't get to where I wanted to go unless I moved myself down in terms of compensation and status. But that's what I did," he added.[70]

Taking a chance, Herman left the area that had distinguished him as a success to follow his dream. For him, it was a new "Day One" of his own making.

You may find that to follow your dream, you have to take a step back before you can leap forward in another direction. It takes courage and confidence to make this move, but the payoff in your long-term happiness and success is worth it.

The Sources of Your Success

As you move along your career path, keep in mind that your job isn't the only source of your success and satisfaction. When you read those words, do you really believe them? Or do you think that, for you, the directional arrow points one way: up? Even if you're a high achiever, know that a job title and salary alone won't bring you satisfaction—not for the longterm, anyway.

Having enjoyed a successful corporate career, and now in the midst of a post-retirement career as a professor, I can tell you that true success is the result of having a balanced life. Only you can decide what makes up that balance in your life. It may be career and family. It may be career, friends, and outside interests. It may even include a spiritual practice. Whatever provides you with greater balance will enhance your life and help you achieve more satisfying and longer-lasting success. If all your satisfaction is derived from one place—your career—you may very well find that your life is out of balance. Moreover, a major disappointment in your professional life can be devastating, and all because you don't derive enough pleasure and satisfaction from other areas of your life. However, if you are fully engaged in several different areas of your life, if you experience a disappointment in one, you have the others to fall back on.

"What I have come to believe very much is that it's a matter of encouraging each individual to march to the tune of his or her own drummer," Bill Bowen added. "Here's an example from my current situation. I am an incorrigible seven-day-a-week worker. I enjoy what I do. I am very privileged that there is no line between work and play for me. However, I have a wonderful young colleague who is extremely able and talented, who has a young family and strong interests in his church and community. So I've gone to great pains to explain to him not to work my schedule, but rather to work the schedule that suits him and his family. That is a crucial point, because there is no one-size-fits-all solution. You need to find the balance that works for you based on your life, your age, your family responsibilities, and your interests. You can't be mechanical about it, because there isn't one formula."[71]

For Andrea Jung, chairman of Avon Products and the mother of two, balance is not accomplished day by day, but rather over time. "You can't have it all in a day," she reflected. "There are absolutely days that Avon loses, and there are absolutely days that my children lose. But it's never on the most important days for Avon or on the most important days for my children. I will always be at the most important meeting for Avon and at the most important recital or game for my children. You can't do it 10 days out of 10. You do it 6 out of 10—but make sure that it's the right 6."

Whether you're striking the balance between work and family, a personal life, or an outside interest, it's all about making the right choices for the quality of your life. "That is the glass being half full," Andrea continued. "Yes, there will be things that you will miss. But at the end of the day, it becomes a freedom, knowing that I don't have to do 10 out of 10."[72]

While a diversified life requires a balancing act, it does make you a more interesting person whom others will want to get to know. Some of the most boring people you'll ever meet are workaholics who can only talk about what they do. If you feel like you run the risk of having a one-dimensional life in which you derive all your joy and satisfaction from one source—be it your job, your marriage, your hobby—take note. A little balance goes a long way, helping to alleviate stress and provide you with a different perspective that can even make you more effective in your life and work. With balance also comes the opportunity to enjoy long-term, enduring success in many areas of your life.

Nell Minow leads a diversified life, wearing two distinctly different hats: as editor of The Corporate Library, an independent research firm providing corporate governance data, and as a movie critic for Yahoo.com. An attorney by training who spent many years working in government, Nell says her two jobs are "actually one vocation."

"They are both just different kinds of systems analysis. Even before I had these two jobs, when I was in government, I was looking at regulatory programs—when they work and when they don't. I have always been interested in why things didn't work," Nell commented.

Both her jobs, she's quick to add, also met the three criteria that have governed her life and career for more than 20 years, ensuring that she kept a vitally important balance between work and her personal life.

"The first thing for me, which was absolutely nonnegotiable, was that I work no more than three days a week. If I did not do that, I could not have a happy family," explained Nell, now the mother of two college-age children. The second consideration, she said, was "to learn something new all the time. I like to multitask." Third, "I had to feel like I was on the side of the good guys. I need to help make the world a better place. So I needed to have fun and work at something that makes a difference."

In addition to her two busy careers, Nell has been very active as a volunteer in various community organizations, which she calls "indispensable" at any stage of life. "If you don't do that (volunteer work), you don't have a full life," she observed. "I think you should do a range of things, some that is very community-oriented; I did Cub Scouts and Girl Scouts. Later, consider some volunteer work that has a broader reach. I think that's crucial." If you're still in college or just launching your career, volunteering and doing "good works" may be something you envision doing later, after you've established your career. Who knows! Maybe you think you won't do that until you retire. Right now you are just too busy to do anything beyond your job. The problem, however, is that if you aren't careful, your work life can absorb you to the exclusion of everything else. That won't make you more successful; in fact, it could work against you. Having meaningful outside interests will make your life more balanced and will give you a richer context and a break from the nose-to-the-grindstone routine of work.

"Deciding to do volunteer work later? That's baloney. You have to do it all the time. That was a lesson I learned from my parents, who were extremely busy people, and yet who were involved in every good civic work in Chicago—and we still had dinner together every night. I could see that it was their volunteer work that made their eyes light up. They set a good example," Nell said.[73]

The value of volunteer work extends beyond just doing "good work" to knowing that you have really made a difference to your community, an organization, or a cause that you feel very strongly about. This can lead to enormous satisfaction, helping to balance the disappointments that you may face in your professional life, and amplifying the success you reap over the long run in your career. Success, like happiness, does not come from a single source. Rather, enduring success comes from a life well lived.

Enduring Success

Laura Nash, a senior research fellow, and Howard Stevenson, the Sarofim-Rock Professor of Business Administration at Harvard Business School, researched the components of what they called "real, enduring success," which they defined as "rewards that are sustainable for you and those you care about." Through interviews and observations, Nash and Stevenson concluded that success is "more than a heart-pounding race to the finish line."

"Our research uncovered four irreducible components of enduring success: happiness (feelings of pleasure or contentment about your life); achievement (accomplishments that compare favorably against similar goals others have strived for); significance (the sense that you've made a positive impact on people you care about); and legacy (a way to establish your values or accomplishments so as to help others find future success)," they wrote.[74]

Of these four components of success, happiness and achievement are the ones that draw most people, especially early in their careers. They want to be happy (who doesn't, after all?), and they want to achieve their goals and reap rewards. These are normal and healthy motivations. But they are not the only definitions of success, even for the young professional. The other two components—significance and legacy—are important at any age or stage of your career.

Significance can be defined as the ability to make a difference to those around you. In your work life, you may achieve this by being a team player who genuinely cares about others, or as a manager who truly wants to challenge and develop the people on his or her team. In the thick of things, however, it is so easy to get caught up in the process of running a business. With project deadlines, production schedules, goals, and initiatives, your job can consume your attention. The need to stay focused on what is happening now may keep you from stepping back and thinking about the proverbial big picture. Nonetheless, if you only think about getting the job done—even doing the job well—you have missed the chance for significance.

Production quotas, quality control standards, project deadlines, and so forth are vitally important, and they may be the measure of your productivity. They are not, however, the source of your significance. That is reserved for the people you help, influence, and inspire along the way.

The fourth component of legacy may seem like a topic that's best left for your retirement. It may seem difficult or even absurd for a young professional to contemplate the legacy that he or she will leave behind. It's never too early, however, to consider the legacy that you build day by day. Throughout your career, you will also benefit from the legacy that others have left behind for you. It may be a person you've admired, or a lesson that someone took the time to teach you. It may be an experience as a young professional that you carry with you the rest of your life. It may be something so profound that, many years later, it continues to have an impact.

A Legacy of Being Nice

One of the people who exemplified the power of one's legacy for me over the years was Ron Burton. I first met Ron when we were undergraduates together. He was also a consensus All-American football player and was the first draft choice of the newly established Boston Patriots professional football team. After graduation he went on to have an unbelievable career at John Hancock, first as an outstanding sales executive and later as a motivational speaker addressing young people on the dangers of drinking, smoking, and doing drugs and the importance of family. Ron and I remained close friends over the years until his death from cancer in the fall of 2003.

Ron talked about life and what's important. He underscored the concepts of treating everyone equally and serving the greater good. I can tell you from experience that Ron lived those principles. He had a simple catchphrase that he would share with students in guest lectures. He'd say, "People like nice people. Others will migrate toward a nice person."

The students would always question him: How can you be nice to everyone? Don't they take advantage of you?

Ron's reply: "Only once." If someone tried to take advantage of him, he had no feeling of retaliation, no need to get revenge. Rather, he could recognize the problem and its source: the other person.

Ron's message continues to have an impact to this day, with the people he touched, the way he conducted himself, and the stories he shared. His legacy lives on with the Ron Burton Training Village, a 300-acre camp outside Boston, Mass. Its mission is to build self-esteem, self-reliance, respect for others, and racial harmony through athletic and educational activities for middle and high school-age boys from inner-city neighborhoods in Massachusetts and other states nationwide. Because of his personal commitment, Ron left an indelible positive mark on the lives of underprivileged youths, many of whom went on to have successful careers of their own.

Your actions, decisions, and interactions with others will compose the legacy you leave behind. With forethought and purpose, you can ensure that your legacy from Day One reflects your commitment to do your best for the organization and for others who work with you and for you. This is a long-term investment in others that will pay rewards to you over time. Even if you leave an organization, the impact you leave behind is the legacy that lives on. If an organization can operate better because you were there, you have made a powerful impact. Others' legacy to you is the lasting influence they have on your life.

"Smile More Than Anyone Else"

Thomas O. Ryder is a success by anyone's standards. Chairman and chief executive officer of The Reader's Digest Association, Inc., Tom attributes his success to three simple statements, which he calls

"Ryder's Rules for Guaranteed Success." (See Chapter 7, "Developing Your Career.")

In addition to the first two rules, "Work harder than anybody else" and "Do the dirty jobs no one else wants to do," Tom's third rule is "Smile more than anybody else." Tom learned that lesson many years ago from a man named Shorty Morris, who worked with him on the Missouri Pacific Railroad back when Tom was entering college.

"Our job was tearing up concrete with jackhammers. It was an eight-hour job," Tom recalls. "I was playing football at the time and was in good condition. Shorty was 62 or 63 years old. When I came on the job, I lasted about 30 minutes before I had to take a breather. Shorty was the kind of guy who didn't stop, and he smiled all through the job."

Working with Shorty that summer before going off to college, Tom learned the value of hard work, setting and keeping commitments, and smiling all the while. "Shorty used to say, 'If you take a man's money, you give him a day of work.' He would never cheat on the breaks. It was a 15-minute break and then back with the hammer," Tom explained. "This was a guy who worked all his life for minimum wage, and he had an impeccable ethical sense about his work."[75]

That was the legacy Shorty Morris left for young Tom Ryder, who never forgot the lesson and applied it throughout his career.

Early Lessons from a First Mentor

The legacy you reap from others may also be the result of someone taking the time to mentor you. That was the experience of Frank LaFasto, who today is senior vice president of organizational effectiveness for Cardinal Health. Back in the late 1970s, when Frank was on the second day of his job at American Hospital Supply (which was later bought by Baxter Healthcare), he met one of the top executives. He was, as Frank recalled, "my boss's boss's boss!"

Frank walked up and introduced himself. "Please call me Brien," the executive said, and eagerly engaged Frank in conversation. "I told him that I was new with the corporation and wanted to know if he had any suggestions of how I could best make a contribution," Frank recalled.

The executive's advice was to find a drugstore nearby, stand by the entrance, and hold the door open for 10 people. "He told me, 'I'd like you to observe a couple of things: how many people say thank you and how many don't. Then observe the people themselves. What do you notice about those who say thank you and those who don't?' When I finished this assignment, he told me to call him," Frank explained.

Frank did as Brien suggested then called him. "I told him that six said thank you and four did not," Frank continued. "Those who said thank you seemed to be smiling. They were better groomed, and they didn't appear to be preoccupied with themselves. Those who didn't were more rough around the edges and seemed a little into themselves."

Asked about how he felt about the ones who said thank you, Frank said that he obviously felt better about those who did.

Then Brien gave him advice that Frank took to heart: "He told me, 'Whatever you decide to do, I want you to remember the two most important words in the world—thank you. People who know those two words go further.' That was a piece of feedback about what I could do to make a contribution that made an indelible impression on me. I can tell you that I've raised five children, and I've taught them that lesson. It's made a difference in how I approach humanity."[76]

Doing Things Right

The legacies that others leave for you may not seem like such a big deal at the time, but upon reflection you realize their impact. That's certainly the case with my job at the gas station when I was about 16. My family wasn't wealthy, so I was always looking for a part-time job while I was in high school. When I was hired at the gas station, my job was pumping gas (there was no self-serve in those days), checking the oil, and washing the windshield. My boss was a fanatic when it came to windshields. After I would wash a customer's windshield, he would come out and inspect it with his eyes right up against the glass.

"It's not clean," he'd tell me, even though it looked awfully clean to me. But the windshield had tiny specks that were only visible close up. "If you're going to do a job, do it right."

I had heard that advice before, but this time I really took it to heart. From then on, my goal was to do a job to the very best of my ability and make sure the final product was as good as it could be. Sometimes that really impressed a customer. When 16-year-old Jane Schulte drove up to the station in her parents' car and said, "Fill it up!," I put the gas pump in for 30 seconds before gas started squirting out.

"I don't think you need any gas," I told her. The gas tank was full when she came in. I washed the windshield, and I did an excellent job, if I say so myself. Jane must have been impressed. We've been married 45 years.

"Help Your Rivals"

Don't overlook the value of lessons you'll gain in your day-to-day interactions with your peers. Even a competitor vying for the same promotion can teach you about true leadership and healthy competition. One of the lessons that Tom Ryder learned through the course of his career was "help your rivals." Although it seems counterintuitive, this lesson increased his contribution both inside and outside the company. In his early 20s, Tom and another young professional named Fred were rivals for their mentor's attention and for the next job. They were pitted against each other to goad them into better performance. Tom, however, wasn't comfortable with the dynamic and decided to do something radically different.

"I decided that if I helped Fred, the rivalry could not exist. I bent over backwards to help him achieve things that were part of our common goals. It changed the relationship," Tom recalled. "What had been a rivalry became an intense friendship. Let me tell you, that was one of the best organizations that I ever worked in. There is a team of people who still have an annual reunion every year—that's how close we were."[77]

As you build your legacy, be conscious of the things of which you are the most proud. It may be the project that was on time and under budget, or the initiative that you championed from concept to completion. Or it may be the potential "star" you spotted on your team whom you coached and developed, who later went on to a high-level position in the organization.

In your life and career, the people you influence and those who leave a lasting impact on you should be many and varied. They should be like flowers in a garden, perennials that bloom and grow year after year, each beautiful and unique in its own way.

Disappointments and Missed Opportunities

As much as you'd like to focus on your achievements and accomplishments, you will have your share of disappointments, setbacks, and missed opportunities. With the passage of time, you may find yourself lamenting the missed opportunities, the bad decisions, and the wrong turns you've made along the way. No one is exempt from these feelings. If you—or someone else—can learn something from your mistakes, even if they had disastrous consequences, it's not a total loss.

Know that you can only make decisions based on the knowledge and perspective you have at the time. If you turn down something that ends up being a big winner, well, that's life. Know what your reasons were and why you made that decision at the time. If nothing else, you'll have a good story to tell.

Opportunities Missed?

One day, I received a phone call from a friend with a clothing company in Baltimore. Given my background, there was someone he wanted me to meet.

"I have this acquaintance," he told me, "a young designer, about your age, who has great taste and a sense of style. But he doesn't have your expertise in operations. He and his uncle are starting a business in Brooklyn, and I think you two could be a good match."

He gave me Ralph Lipschitz's phone number, and I called him. We conversed at length. I learned more about his operation, which was really a family business. Ralph and I talked for a while, and it seemed like an intriguing idea. But by this time, I had four young kids. I didn't want to uproot them and move them to Brooklyn to work at a clothing startup with Ralph.

His business, I should mention, was called Polo.

I turned down Ralph Lipschitz, later known as Ralph Lauren. He was a very nice guy with whom I could have easily worked. I just didn't think that decision was the best for my life at the time. Did I throw away a valuable opportunity? In hindsight it sure seems like it, but at the time I made the decision based on my career, my life, and my family.

When you are faced with personal and professional setbacks, look for the big picture in terms of long-term, broad-based goals. Short-term, specific goals are pretty meaningless, because circumstances are always changing. Focusing on them can mean one disappointment after another. But if you have a vision of where you want to be, which is less specific about the steps along the way, you have a greater chance to achieve what you set out to accomplish.

While it's easy to become absorbed in the tasks at hand and the responsibilities you shoulder, you can gain the necessary psychological or spiritual perspective only by taking a step back and away from work. Nell Minow recalled that, while she and her husband were law students at the University of Chicago, they decided to "play hooky" to enjoy a beautiful spring day. Upon returning to campus, they ran into a classmate, one of the top students, who was coming out of the library, where he had spent the entire day. "When we told him what we had done, he said, 'There will be beautiful days when I become a partner.' That was so sad. If you believe that, then you give away part of your soul," she commented.

"You have to be a complete person, to make space for friends and family and volunteer activities, for going to the theater and to concerts. In addition to fulfilling your life, they will make you better at what your job is," Nell added. "There is a terrible trap out there about working long hours. The truth is, most people manage their time very badly and they are not that effective. If you are working seven days a week, you're not an effective worker or a complete person."[78]

Disappointments can also have their own positive payback, in ways that you may not have initially anticipated. It may be that, in taking a risk to try something that did not work out as you planned, you gained insight into yourself.

Herman Cain—successful businessman, author, and motivational speaker—was encouraged to seek public office, and he became a candidate for the U.S. Senate from Georgia. He had already proven himself to be unafraid of taking risks, such as when he made a dramatic career change at age 34. Running for the Senate, he was willing to take a risk again. While he was not ultimately victorious, his first foray into politics was hardly a failure, as Herman sees it. "That race has become a springboard to things I never considered before. Other opportunities have come about that are just as important as having won the race," he observed.[79]

He is now in a position to consider those opportunities because he was willing to take a risk and embrace another Day One at an age when many successful executives would be glad to rest on their laurels and retire quietly.

Giving Back

At some point in your career, you will need to consider your obligation to give back. This will be part of your legacy as well. You can accomplish this in small ways, such as mentoring a new colleague, or in big ways, such as becoming actively involved in community work or a charity.

For you too, every time you recommit to your personal and professional path, every time you revisit your priorities and evaluate the contribution you are making, it is a new Day One.

SUCCESS SECRETS

➤ Genuine success is enduring.

➤ A balanced life cushions the inevitable disappointments and amplifies your accomplishments.

➤ Be conscious of the legacy you build From Day One.

Appendix

YOUR TOOLBOX FOR SUCCESS

Do you wonder how or why people get ahead? Why are they chosen for schools, picked for clubs, drafted onto teams, or put into business leadership positions? Have you noticed that often it's not the smartest person or the one who has accomplished the most who succeeds?

What, then, is the secret to this success? Is it networking? Personal work ethic? Emotional intelligence? I believe it's a combination of these factors, plus a few more of what I call the Fundamental Habits for Success. These qualities and skills are derived from abilities and habits you already have—reading, writing, speaking, listening—and they complement others you have developed, such as understanding other people's emotions and controlling your own. Combined, these skills and behaviors are important tools to use from Day One and throughout your career.

At the core of these skills are the Fundamental Habits for Success. As you read the following list, you'll see that none seems revolutionary. You've been listening and speaking since long before you could tie your shoes! These basic human skills, however, can be elevated to an art form. This will improve your retention of what is being said, increase your understanding of what is truly important and germane to the situation, and allow you to speak in such a way as to command respect.

Fundamental Habits for Success

- **Reading:** Broad-based and eclectic, including things you don't agree with

- **Writing:** Logically, emotionally, naturally

- **Speaking:** Confidently, with integrity

- **Listening:** Segmenting your brain to keep engaged; asking "therapist questions"

- **Prioritizing**: Implementing time-management strategies

- **Estimating:** Employing practical discernment

- **Forecasting:** Making predictions and gauging impacts

Reading: You Are What You Read

Successful people read very widely. They are very eclectic readers with interests that span a great many fields. Among their reading materials, however, are a few common elements. For one, they read the best newspaper in the country, wherever they happen to be living and working. In the United States, the best newspaper, I believe, is the *New York Times*, because the vast majority of the material in the *Times* is original reporting. Only a small percentage of the content has been picked up from wire service reports or other sources. This isn't true of many other large and respected newspapers.

The second thing on your reading list should be the largest circulation newspaper in your city. This is essential for any manager for the simple reason that this is the newspaper that people working for you are reading. If you want to know what affects their lives, what interests them, and what they are thinking about, read the local newspaper.

Third, read things you don't agree with. While you can't do this as a steady diet, it is important to expand your mind and your point of view by purposefully reading articles, columns, and editorials that are of the opinion opposite of yours. For example, if you're in business, read the union newspaper. Approach it with an open mind and a willingness to understand opposing viewpoints and how they are presented.

At this point, you may be saying to, "I don't have time to read all that!" So here's the answer: If you can't read everything in the paper, just read the front page. Newspapers employ very accomplished and well-paid editors who decide what goes on the front page. You can trust their judgment to keep you informed.

Clipping goes hand-in-hand with reading. When you come across an article you think someone else would like, or that you will probably find useful in the future, clip it. (If you read newspapers and magazines online, the same ideas apply. Printouts, emails to yourself or others, and electronic bookmarks will help you build your own files.)

What happens when you come across an article you think your boss would like? Do you just send a note that says, "Here's an article about that technology/concept/idea/whatever you discussed yesterday."? Or do you say something like, "Thought you might find this interesting." Or do you use one of those standard "For Your Information" notes? Take a second look at these possibilities. These comments may look innocuous, but your boss could perceive them as presumptuous on your part and maybe even a little condescending. So what should you do—forego the clipping altogether?

My mentor, Professor Doriot, made a simple suggestion: Attach a note that says "In case you missed this." That's it. Write it. Email it. Attach it. The words "in case you missed this" assume that the recipient is knowledgeable and well-read, and you appear to be thoughtful and helpful. No one could be offended by that, and you won't appear foolish, no matter who gets the note.

Writing: The Power of the Written Word

When you are a manager, you will probably get monthly reports from your direct reports. With a stack of eight or nine of these reports to go through, which would you read first? The one that discussed the most pressing problems at the company? The shortest? The longest? The top choice is often the best-written, for two reasons: First, you can get through them right away and be left with the feeling that the manager of that particular unit or division is doing a good job of dealing with the situation at hand. Second, well-written reports are interesting and inherently logical, making them easy to follow.

Too often people in the business world think that volume impresses people. They think that if they write a 20-page report, they'll look smarter and more impressive than if they write only five pages. But it depends. Does it really take 20 pages to explain all your points? I doubt it. Procter & Gamble used to have a one-page rule. All proposals, notes, and other communiqués had to be kept to one page.

Don't confuse brevity with speed. Often it takes a lot longer to write a succinct report than it does a long, rambling one. It may be harder to write succinctly, but it's certainly easier on the reader. In the wise words of President Harry S Truman, "Never use two words when one will do best."[80]

Business reports can be humorous, but you have to be careful about not making light of the wrong subject. Don't be afraid of putting emotion into them; let the reader know you care about the topic. The best thing you can do when you write is to have it sound like you talk—flowing, conversational, engaging.

In your business emails, you can no longer write with the same offhanded style and shorthand that you used with your friends and classmates. Using B/C and little smiley faces is probably not appropriate for a business email. Think of style and protocol before you start typing. Also keep in mind that it's very easy, in a two-line email, to come across as arrogant, demanding, or smart-alecky. After you write an email, take a moment to read it one more time before clicking Send, because once it's gone, you can't get it back! Plus, it could be forwarded to many more people.

One more note about writing. Handwritten notes make an impact. Yes, it is far easier to dash off a quick email or to click Reply and toss a few lines to someone. But does that really make an impact? Are you really making the person feel special? To show others that they matter, send a handwritten note on good stationery, preferably monogrammed. Amy Vanderbilt, the doyenne of etiquette, used to call these thank-you notes "bread and butter letters," one of the basics of good manners.[51]

If you are wondering when you might employ this bread-and-butter letter strategy, consider it when you are interviewing for a job. The conventional means is to respond via email to thank the interviewer for taking the time to meet with you and to express your interest in the job. I suggest that you take that standard reply to a higher level by sending a handwritten note on good stationery. While this may seem old-fashioned, handwritten notes are so "out" that they're "in." Interviewers will be pleasantly surprised by your effort and will remember you.

Speaking: Mastering the Spoken Word

Become comfortable with speaking in public. Take a public-speaking course. Toastmasters is inexpensive and relatively painless, and you can find one almost anywhere. Do what you have to do to become more at ease speaking in front of a group. Learn to speak well, with emotion and persuasion.

In informal speaking, it's important to know when to speak and when not to. For those starting out in business, this can be a very tricky judgment call. Not wanting to say something inappropriate, you say nothing at all. Not wanting to be overlooked, you speak up freely. How do you know what to do? My best advice is to observe what's going on around you. Pick up the tone and undercurrents of the business meeting. If someone else speaks out in what appears to be an argumentative tone, and you can see a negative reaction from others, file it away for yourself. That's not how you want to participate. However, if a free-flowing discussion is under way, and people who speak out with emotion and conviction are heard and respected—even if they voice a contrary view—note that too.

In the business world, each of us has a certain number of "chips" or credits, if you will, that allow us to make a mistake or speak out of turn and be indulged or forgiven. Your supply of chips, however, is not inexhaustible, although they do regenerate with time. Knowing that, you should be more confident about speaking out when you feel strongly. If the discussion is going off on a wrong tangent, away from the critical main point, and you feel absolutely confident that you are right, speak up and say so. But don't make a habit of it, or you may find that you won't be invited to the next meeting, or people will begin to question whether you are a good fit with the organization. You may even question it yourself.

If you are having the feeling too frequently that things are going in the wrong direction, perhaps you are in the wrong organization. If this is the case, you'll have to plan your transition to doing something else. The organization's values will not change.

The one area in which you must always speak up is ethics. If an ethical issue comes up, and you are taken aback by the tone of the discussion or the decisions that are being talked about or made, you should stand up and say something like "I don't like where this discussion is going." Then leave the room. If you are uncomfortable with such a bold public statement, just make a fuss when you get up and leave. Whatever you do, a visible exit will get your point across. Even if it costs you your next promotion, or you lose your job, you cannot sit silently in the face of a serious breach of ethics. Otherwise, you can never see yourself (or be seen by others) as an ethical person. That's one compromise you can never make.

Another key point is asking questions. In general, your goal should be to ask open-ended questions that invite explanation and discussion rather than closed questions that can be answered with a quick "yes" or "no." When asking open-ended questions, you must be mindful of two important factors: the content and the emotion. The content is what you are looking to ascertain, and the emotion reveals your motivation. For example, if you are double-checking something—the expected deadline, some fact that was mentioned earlier, and so forth—your question should be without emotion.

A good strategy is to phrase a question in such a way that the other person does not feel challenged at all, but rather is invited to give feedback. For example, let's say you want to get an update on an ongoing project. Rather than asking, "Is the project on time?"—even if you suspect that it won't meet the deadline—try a more subtle approach. "Were you pleased with the results of this phase of the project?" Phrasing the question this way assumes that the project is on schedule. If it is, the other person has been invited to discuss the preliminary findings or give an update on what's happening thus far. If the project is behind schedule, the respondent may be embarrassed but clearly will get the message.

On the other hand, let's say you want to find out if someone is truly committed—emotionally as well as financially—to completing a project. Sensing that the person's commitment is weak or wavering, you might take a reverse tactic with a question such as "How would you feel if we just canceled the project right now?" Using this reverse questioning, you will soon find out if that person is willing to stand up and fight for the project. One way or another, you'll know if the project is likely to proceed or be canceled, without directly calling into question the person's commitment to it.

The art of asking questions is developed with practice, not only by doing but also by observing. As others ask questions, look for the feedback that goes beyond the answer that's given. For example, does the person act defensive? Is the question answered thoroughly or brushed off? What's important, though, is to recognize that feedback and interpret it. Even if this doesn't come naturally to you, it is a habit that can be developed.

When it comes to asking questions and being part of a group discussion, don't underestimate the impact of silence. Listen. Observe. Absorb.

A final note on speaking: beware if you have fallen into the trap of college-speak. It's essential that, as a new professional, you use terminology that's generally accepted in your new organization. Avoid "awesome" and know that the word "like" is used to describe something, not as an extra adjective that can be thrown in at random.

Listening: A (Nearly) Lost Art

Listening is not a passive endeavor. It requires discipline and the full commitment of your brainpower. The problem, however, is that when you listen to someone speaking, whether in a meeting, in a classroom, or when a speech is given, you can keep up with him or her using a small portion of your brain. The rest of your brain is free to wander to other topics, whether it's lunch, the weekend, your girlfriend/boyfriend, or your next vacation. The problem, obviously, is that these other thoughts can distract you to the point that you don't retain the important information that is being presented.

How, then, can you become a better listener? One way is to actively engage your brain while you are listening. Use that "spare capacity" to anticipate the next point, to ask mental questions about why the speaker said something and not something else. Observe what the speaker has said and where he or she might be going next. Few people do this well. But once you have mastered it, the speaker can see it in your eyes. Your expression reflects a mind that is engaged, not a blank stare. Remember, it's very hard to be tuned into speakers if you don't look at them. Active listening also leads to accurate listening.

Developing your listening skills will also help you with a common problem: remembering names. Many successful executives are known for this ability. Several techniques can help you remember names. The first is to repeat the name as soon as possible. Second, tell yourself that this is something you want to remember, and, if possible, link it to a visual image that helps you recall the name.

As you fine-tune your listening skills in the business world, know that there's no such thing as an unimportant comment by the boss, particularly a high-ranking one. If your boss makes a comment, take note. If the boss's boss says something, really pay attention. Most bosses do (and all of them should) choose their words carefully because of the problem of amplification—when a few casual words are taken out of context and blown out of proportion. When you're the CEO, you can't make an off-the-cuff remark and expect others to shrug it off, because people hang on to every word the top leader says. Even a comment that's made lightly can get amplified and spark actions that are not only unexpected, but possibly unwelcome. (Keep that in mind too as you are promoted and take on positions of increasing authority.)

How do you get to be a better listener, particularly in one-on-one situations? Pretend that you're a therapist, asking questions of a client. Between comments, let there be momentary silence. Don't jump in with your own words to fill the void. Use inviting comments such as "So…" or "Yes…" Using the power of silence will encourage the person to provide more information and details, and it will give the positive impression that you're really listening to what's being said.

Prioritizing: Managing Your Time Wisely

When priorities change or demands shift, you will need to be flexible enough to refocus your attention and reprioritize your tasks and responsibilities. To do this successfully, you will need to assess your time-management skills. You may need to shift your focus when an urgent task or project suddenly preempts what you've been doing. You may be working in an environment, such as a consulting firm, where you are expected to do whatever it takes to get the job done— even if it means working nights and weekends.

At other firms, you may be able to get help to complete the project. Or you may be able to approach your boss with a plan on how to reprioritize the work. Don't look for your boss to sort it all out for you, though. Explain what you can accomplish on deadline and what you can put off for a while. Even if the boss disagrees with you and shifts your priorities, you will demonstrate that you can prioritize tasks and that you're not afraid to seek help.

One technique for improving your time management is to watch out for potential pitfalls that can sabotage your efforts to be efficient and responsive. For example, if you tend to be a perfectionist, your work habits can get in the way of knowing when something is "good enough." (If you are creative or have artistic inclinations, you may have this problem. You know from experience that you can tinker with a phrase, color, or design endlessly, only to end up back where you started.) You need the discipline to know when to stop in order to turn in good work on time and to shift to the next project.

Extreme perfectionists also fall into a category of people known as "time abusers," for whom routine organization techniques don't work. According to Steven Berglas, a clinical psychologist and executive coach, time abusers include, in addition to perfectionists, "preemptives," who turn in their work ahead of time to stay in control but who are not good team players; "people pleasers," who can't say no to others and end up taking on too much; and "procrastinators," who put off as much as possible. The real issues with these time abusers, Berglas says, are "brittle self-esteem and an unconscious fear of being evaluated and found wanting." His advice for time abusers, and the bosses who manage them, is to find out what makes them anxious, instead of teaching them to organize their day.[82]

Another key time management skill is multitasking, which means being able to put aside one project to take up another and then return to the first one. Some people by nature can do this better than others. If you multitask easily, you are a "parallel." It's easy for you to keep tabs on more than one thing at a time, and you can switch from one thing to another easily. If multitasking is more difficult, you may be a "serial." Your preference is to work on one thing at a time, concluding each task before starting another.

Some drawbacks exist to being a serial, though, which could hamper your career later. General managers, I believe, are typically parallels, able to multitask many things and keep track of multiple responsibilities. If you are a serial who can't (or doesn't want to) try to become more parallel, you may be more comfortable with staff positions and projects.

The last consideration about time management is to consider your responsiveness. Instant messaging. Email. A cell phone in everybody's pocket. We live in a world of immediate access. But not every communiqué is urgent, and if you immediately reply to every email, you may have difficulty getting your work done. One way to tackle this problem is to devote specific blocks of time to read and reply to email. Respond to your email based on the message's urgency and priority. Another trick is to deal with each email only once. If you leave it hanging, you'll waste time rereading needlessly. Certainly be responsive and reliable, answering email and voicemail within a day. But don't be so glued to your email that it gets in the way of your ability to focus on your work.

Estimating: Is It $2 Million, $20 Million, or $200 Million?

This scenario happens far more often than you think, particularly in business when someone is asked to write a report that includes some calculations. "The production line's full capacity is 40,000 units a day, which would result in maximum output of 12 million a month..." What? The real answer (40,000 units times 30 days a month) is 1.2 million. The decimal point was simply in the wrong place.

While this error is easy to detect, think about what can happen with far more complex calculations. That's why estimating is important, to make the numbers more relevant and logical before you do the calculation. Using this basic example, if a production line could make 40,000 units a day, that's 280,000 in seven days—a little over a quarter million a week. Since a month has four weeks, that means the answer will be a million and change. If you did the calculation and came up with an answer of 12 million, you'd know that something was wrong. You'd go back through your math and find the errant decimal.

Practice with things around you. Next time you take a drive, estimate how long it should take you to get from one place to the next based on the distance and your speed. Make mental calculations, and double check them with your math. Estimating will keep you from making errors that you wish you hadn't.

Forecasting: What's Your Prediction?

When something occurs, how often do you hear somebody say, "I knew that would happen"? Maybe you say it yourself. But did you really expect that outcome or result? Forecasting is an important skill that you will employ not only in business, but also in your personal life.

One of the most important areas to forecast is predetermining how you expect people will react when you unexpectedly announce a decision. Granted, in the earliest stages of your career, you may not be making many of these kinds of decisions. But even when you become a low-level manager, you should devote time and effort to anticipating how specific employees will react to something. Based on your predictions, you can plot out your communication plan accordingly. Once you've made the announcement, you can determine how accurate your forecasts were compared with the actual reactions. This will tell you how skilled you are at making these interpersonal predictions.

Peter F. Drucker, the renowned management expert, takes a complementary approach to forecasting, which he calls "feedback analysis." "Whenever you make a key decision or take a key action, write down what you expect will happen," Drucker advised. "Nine or 12 months later, compare the actual results with your expectations. I have been practicing this method for 15 to 20 years now, and every time I do it, I am surprised. The feedback analysis showed me, for instance—and to my great surprise—that I have an intuitive understanding of technical people, whether they are engineers or accountants or market researchers. It also showed me that I don't really resonate with generalists."[53]

Like Drucker, you may also uncover some hidden talents when it comes to forecasting. For example, as you practice predicting outcomes in terms of people's reactions, you may also test your skills at studying and forecasting trends that are related to your job. You may find, for example, that you are good at forecasting the future price of a commodity (be it oil or soybeans), but you aren't as good at determining the outcome of opening two factories. Even if this kind of decision-making isn't part of your job right now, you can still practice. Determining how accurate you are at forecasting particular events and outcomes will help you see the type of business area you might pursue.

Your Emotional Habits for Success

In addition to the Fundamental Habits for Success, additional skills and habits can enhance your ability to do the job and make a contribution. They are the Emotional Habits for Success. At the top of the list is "emotional intelligence," which has been widely discussed over the years, and which remains highly relevant today.

Two psychologists, John "Jack" Mayer, Ph.D. of the University of New Hampshire and Peter Salovey, Ph.D. of Yale University, are credited with early work on emotional intelligence. They defined it as the "ability to monitor one's own and others' feelings and emotions, to discriminate among them, and to use this information to guide one's thinking and actions."[84]

Author Daniel Goleman studied emotional intelligence in the business world, concluding that it is vitally important to success. "Emotional intelligence skills are synergistic with cognitive ones; top performers have both. The more complex the job, the more emotional intelligence matters—if only because a deficiency in these abilities can hinder the use of whatever technical expertise or intellect a person may have."[85]

Let's take a look at some business world examples of why emotional intelligence is important. Your boss says that a particular problem or situation is "no big deal." But the boss's emotions, as revealed by his or her facial expression, tone of voice, and body language, indicate something else. The boss is clearly upset by what is going on, but for some reason—personal or political—he or she has chosen to downplay the impact in words.

Or a colleague may be sending signals that he or she is uncomfortable with a conversation. When you ask, "What's wrong?", the person only shrugs and says, "Nothing." Do you believe the words, or should you pay attention to the emotional signals? Becoming astute in reading people will provide you insight between the lines of what is being said, helping you ascertain the "hot buttons" before conflict erupts, and letting you know that far more is occurring below the surface than words indicate.

Controlling Your Emotions

Controlling your emotions is another component of emotional intelligence that will help you be more effective and make a greater positive impact at work. Admittedly, this can be challenging, particularly when you're in a confrontational or stressful situation. Rather than shooting from the hip with a retort or an outburst, a better way to respond is by first calming your body and clearing your mind. Find a way to quiet your racing heart and curb your temper, whether it's counting to ten or taking deep breaths. The point is not to become passive. Rather, your aim is to control your temper and to communicate with appropriate emotion, instead of confronting one adversity after another. Controlling your emotions also will help you read others more clearly.

A highly effective tool to control your emotions is to compartmentalize your thinking. This will help rein in out-of-control fears, anxiety, and stress to keep them from devouring your life. Whether it's a personal issue consuming your business life or the other way around, at times you will feel overwhelmed. In that state of emotional overload, your ability to contribute to your company will be diminished, and you will have far less satisfaction from your daily life.

By compartmentalizing your thinking, however, you literally set aside problems that you cannot deal with at the moment to focus on the issues at hand. You may find that, when you return to the problem, you have more clarity of thought to address it. From a business standpoint, compartmentalizing is a valuable attribute. People who walk around with emotional hangovers and an air of distraction about them may not be viewed favorably, and they could find that they are the last ones to be promoted.

Your emotional intelligence—encompassing your emotional control and well-being, your ability to read others, and your disposition—is important to consider as you enter the business world. Whatever career path you choose, your emotional qualities and attributes will greatly influence how others perceive you, including whether they want to work with you.

As you move forward from Day One, what will make you an important member of the team? To answer that question, go back to your childhood and think about when sides were chosen for teams. Some kids were picked first, and some were chosen last. What made the difference in most cases was the person's ability to play the game. In that regard, things haven't changed all that much.

In the teams to which you are assigned, in the ones you are asked to join, and in the ones you will lead, you can distinguish yourself by using the Fundamental Habits for Success and the Emotional Habits for Success. These behaviors and habits can enhance the talents, skills, expertise, and interest you bring to the job and make you more effective—from Day One and throughout your career.

END NOTES

1. Bogle, John C., founder and former chairman of The Vanguard Group. Telephone interview. August 10, 2004.

2. Maddux, Greg, pitcher for the Chicago Cubs. Telephone interview. August 29, 2004.

3. Bogle, John C.

4. Kelley, Robert E., Carnegie Mellon's Graduate School of Industrial Administration. Telephone interview. July 20, 2004.

5. Lieberman, Pamela Forbes, former president and chief executive officer of TruServ (now known as True Value Company). Telephone interview. July 15, 2004.

6. Jung, Andrea, chairman of Avon Products. Telephone interview. November 23, 2004.

7. "The Top 50 Women to Watch," Wall Street Journal Online, November 8, 2004. http://online.wsj.com (accessed November 8, 2004).

8. Batts, Warren, former CEO of Premark and Tupperware. Telephone interview. July 6, 2004.

9. Jung, Andrea.

10. Batts, Warren.

11. Gray, John D., former CEO of Hart Schaffner & Marx. Telephone interview. July 20, 2004.

12. Jung, Andrea.

13. Bogle, John C.

14. Lieberman, Pamela Forbes.

15. Bowen, William G., president of The Andrew W. Mellon Foundation and former president of Princeton University. Telephone interview. October 6, 2004.

16. Greenleaf, Robert K. *Servant Leadership: A Journey into the Nature of Legitimate Power & Greatness*, 25th Anniversary Edition. New York/Mahwah, N.J.: Paulist Press, 2002.

17. Maddux, Greg.

18. Donovan, John. "Center of Attention: Modest Maddux can't escape spotlight as member of 300 Club," SportsIllustrated.com, August 7, 2004. http://sportsillustrated.cnn.com/2004/writers/john_donovan/08/06/maddux.300/ (accessed February 23, 2005).

19. Gray, John D.

20. Delves, Donald P. *Stock Options & The New Rules of Corporate Accountability: Measuring, Managing, and Rewarding Executive Performance*. New York: McGraw-Hill, 2004.

21. Barr, Peggy, professor emeritus at Northwestern University's School of Education and Social Policy and former vice president of student affairs. Telephone interview. August 17, 2004.

22. Bogle, John C.

23. Tischler, Linda. "Extreme Networking: MBAs Show the Way," *Fast Company*, July 2001.

24. Kelley, Robert E. *How to Be a Star at Work: 9 Breakthrough Strategies You Need to Succeed*. New York: Times Business/Random House, 1998.

25. Kelley, Robert E.

26. Luthans, Fred. "Successful vs. Effective Real Managers," *Academy of Management Executives*, (1988).

27. Lieberman, Pamela Forbes.

28. Barr, Peggy.

29. Lieberman, Pamela Forbes.

30. Jung, Andrea.

31. Citrin, James, senior director of Spencer Stuart. Telephone interview. August 12, 2004.

32. Cain, Herman, former chairman of Godfather's Pizza, CEO and president of T.H.E. Inc. Telephone interview. October 28, 2004.

33. Bell, David E. "Reunion—Reframe the way you think about risk," *Remember Who You Are: Life Stories That Inspire the Heart and Mind*. Edited by Daisy Wademan. Boston: Harvard Business School Press, 2004.

34. Bolles, Richard N. *What Color Is Your Parachute? A Practical Manual for Job-Hunters and Career-Changers*. Berkeley, Calif.: Ten Speed Press, 2005.

35. Citrin, James.

36. Niewoehner, Gerry, corporate psychologist and principal of Niewoehner Associates. Telephone interview. June 23, 2004.

37. Livingston, J. Sterling. "Pygmalion in Management," *Harvard Business Review* (January 2003).

38. Batts, Warren.

39. Delves, Donald P., founder of The Delves Group. Telephone interview. August 17, 2004.

40. Delves, Donald.

41. Citrin, James M. and Richard A. Smith. *The 5 Patterns of Extraordinary Careers: The Guide for Achieving Success and Satisfaction*. New York: Crown Business/Random House, Inc., 2003.

42. Citrin, James.

43. Batts, Warren.

44. Batts, Warren.

45. Batts, Warren.

46. Maddux, Greg.

47. Peters, Thomas J. and Robert H. Waterman, Jr. *In Search of Excellence: Lessons from America's Best-Run Companies*. New York: Harper & Row Publishers, 1982.

48. Wilson, Edmund, associate dean emeritus of the Kellogg School of Management at Northwestern University and former associate dean of MBA programs and student affairs. Telephone interview. October 25, 2004.

49. Cain, Herman.

50. Valdmanis, Thor. "Tuck's MBAs are hot property again," *USA Today* (June 30, 2004).

51. National Public Radio, *Morning Edition*, August 28, 2002. "Interview: Jeffrey Pfeffer on claims made by some business schools to students about well-paying jobs and quick promotions." www.npr.org (accessed May 24, 2004).

52. Wilson, Ed.

53. Badenhausen Kurt, and Lesley Kump. "The Best Business Schools, B-Schools: The Payback," Forbes.com, October 13, 2003. www.forbes.com (accessed July 19, 2004).

54. Wilson, Ed.

55. Cain, Herman.

56. Wilson, Ed.

57. Ryder, Thomas, chairman and chief executive officer of The Reader's Digest Association, Inc. Telephone interview. August 30, 2004.

58. Ryder, Thomas.

59. LaFasto, Frank, senior vice president of organization effectiveness for Cardinal Health. Telephone interview. August 30, 2004.

60. LaFasto, Frank.

61. Walker, Carol A. "Saving Your Rookie Managers from Themselves," *Harvard Business Review* (April 2002).

62. Bowen, William G.

63. Livingston, J. Sterling.

64. Maddux, Greg.

65. Kelley, Robert E.

66. Drucker, Peter F., "Managing Oneself," *Harvard Business Review* (March-April 1999).

67. LaFasto, Frank.

68. Bowen, William G.

69. Bowen, William G.

70. Cain, Herman.

71. Bowen, William G.

72. Jung, Andrea.

73. Minow, Nell, editor of The Corporate Library. Telephone interview. October 14, 2004.

74. Nash, Laura and Howard Stevenson. "Success That Lasts," *Harvard Business Review* (February 2004).

75. Ryder, Thomas.

76. LaFasto, Frank.

77. Ryder, Thomas.

78. Minow, Nell.

79. Cain, Herman.

80. Key, Ralph. *The Wit & Wisdom of Harry Truman: A Treasury of Quotations, Anecdotes, and Observations*. New York: HarperCollins, 1995.

81. Tuckerman, Nancy and Nancy Dunnan. *The Amy Vanderbilt Complete Book of Etiquette: Entirely Rewritten and Updated*. New York: Doubleday, 1995.

82. Berglas, Steven. "Chronic Time Abuse," *Harvard Business Review* (June 2004).

83. Drucker, Peter F.

84. Emotionaliq.org. "Overview of Emotional Intelligence." www.emotionaliq.org/EI.htm (accessed April 18, 2004).

85. Goleman, Daniel. *Working with Emotional Intelligence*. New York: Bantam Books, 1998.

INDEX

The Right Decision Every Time
How to Reach Perfect Clarity on Tough Decisions
BY LUDA KOPEIKINA

The Right Decision Every Time will help you gain unprecedented clarity in all your decision-making, so you can make consistently better decisions—and make them more rapidly. Drawing on her breakthrough MIT research with 115 CEOs, Luda Kopeikina offers practical, proven techniques for structuring decisions, achieving clarity about the real issues involved, and using that clarity to improve the quality of every decision you make. This isn't "one-size-fits-all" decision-making: it's a framework that respects your style and leverages your strengths. Kopeikina begins by defining clarity in decision-making, identifying five root causes for decision difficulty, and introducing the Clarity State: that singular moment of focus where insights are triggered, things fall into place, and solutions become obvious. Next, she introduces a set of powerful techniques for overcoming decision difficulties, stripping away decision complexity, and achieving the Clarity State. Kopeikina concludes with a detailed case study tracing how a real executive used these techniques to make a crucial strategic decision. The book contains a convenient insert summarizing these techniques for easy use "on the road." Using Kopeikina's approach, a stunning 93% of CEOs made clear strategic decisions within 90 minutes or less—even when these decisions had been sitting unresolved for weeks or months. You can be every bit as effective.

ISBN 0131862626, © 2006, 288 pp., $27.99

Winners Never Cheat
Everyday Values We Learned as Children (But May Have Forgotten)
BY JON M. HUNTSMAN

Next time someone tells you business can't be done ethically—corners must be cut, negotiations can't be honest—hand them Jon Huntsman's new book. Who's Jon Huntsman? Just someone who started with practically nothing, and made it to Forbes' list of America's Top 100 richest people. Huntsman is generous about sharing the credit, but in the 21st century, he's the nearest thing to a self-made multi-billionaire. Now, he presents the lessons of a lifetime: a passionate, inspirational manifesto for returning to the days when your word was your bond, a handshake was sacred, and swarms of lawyers weren't needed to back it up. This is no mere exhortation: it's as practical as a business book can get. It's about how you listen to your moral compass, even as others ignore theirs. It's about how you build teams with the highest values...share succes...take responsibility...earn the rewards that only come with giving back. Huntsman has built his career and fortune on these principles—from his youth, refusing the Nixon administration's corrupt demands, to his lifelong commitment to charity, to the way he approaches his biggest deals. You don't live these principles just to "succeed": you live them because they're right. But in an age of non-stop business scandal, Huntsman's life proves honesty is more than right: it's your biggest competitive differentiator. So consider what kind of person you want to do business with. Then be that person—and use this book to get you there.

ISBN 0131863665, © 2005, 224 pp., $19.95